D0690761

creating
a web site in
dreamweaver cs3

Visual QuickProject Guide

by Nolan Hester

**Peachpit
Press**

OCN156951179

Visual QuickProject Guide

Creating a Web Site in Dreamweaver CS3
Nolan Hester

Peachpit Press

1249 Eighth Street
Berkeley, CA 94710
510/524-2178
800/283-9444
510/524-2221 (fax)

Find us on the World Wide Web at: www.peachpit.com
To report errors, please send a note to errata@peachpit.com
Peachpit Press is a division of Pearson Education

Editor: Nancy Davis
Production Editor: David Van Ness
Compositor: David Van Ness
Proofreader: Tracy D. O'Connell
Indexer: FireCrystal Communications
Cover design: Peachpit Press, Aren Howell
Interior design: Elizabeth Castro
Cover photo credit: Rubén Hidalgo / iStock Photo

Notice of Rights

Notice of Liability

Trademarks

ISBN 13: 978-0-321-50304-6
ISBN 10: 0-321-50304-X

9 8 7 6 5 4 3 2 1

Printed and bound in the United States of America

This last one's for Mom.

Special Thanks to...

Nancy Davis, my editor, for making my books way better over the past nine years,

David Van Ness for being such a pro and a rock through 19 books,

Emily Glossbrenner of FireCrystal for always making every index a map of concepts rather than just a vocabulary list,

Marjorie Baer and Cary Norsworthy for helping me get the first edition of this book off the ground,

And, always and forever, Mary.

contents

contents

introduction

The Visual QuickProject Guide that you hold in your hands offers a unique way to learn about new technologies. Instead of drowning you in theoretical possibilities and lengthy explanations, this Visual QuickProject Guide uses big, color illustrations coupled with clear, concise step-by-step instructions to show you how to complete one specific project in a matter of hours.

Our project in this book is to create a beautiful Web site using Adobe Dreamweaver CS3, one of the best programs for building Web sites. Our Web site describes the tours and services of a fictitious travel agency. Because the project covers all the techniques needed to build a basic Web site, you'll be able to use what you learn to create your own Web site. Thanks to Dreamweaver, you'll do all this without having to enter a single line of HTML, the code that drives the Web.

You can use the book two ways. Download the examples at the companion Web site and literally follow each step, chapter by chapter. Or you can create your own site and use the steps as a general guide as you build the items explained in each section and chapter. OK, there's a third way: Use the examples to get your feet wet, and then plunge into building your totally cool site based on what you learn here. Any way you approach it, it'll be fun.

what you'll create

Besides the usual text, headings, and tables, here are some of the things you'll learn to create with Dreamweaver.

Use Cascading Style Sheets to generate clean layouts with site-wide headers, sidebars, and main content areas. (See page 12 and Chapter 6 on page 77.)

Add a variety of images, plus Flash and QuickTime videos, to give pages visual punch. (See pages 27, 29 and 31.)

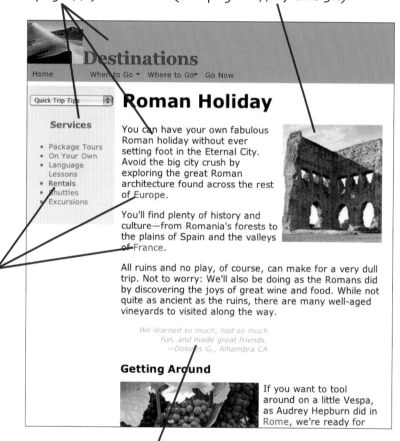

Add internal, external, and email links, then give them a consistent appearance using style sheets. (See Chapter 5 on page 59.)

Create special formats that can be applied to any item, such as pull quotes, and quickly update them anytime. (See page 89.)

Add a jump menu to give visitors a quick view of other items on your site. (See page 99.)

Create an interactive navigation menu to guide visitors as they explore your site. (See page 94.)

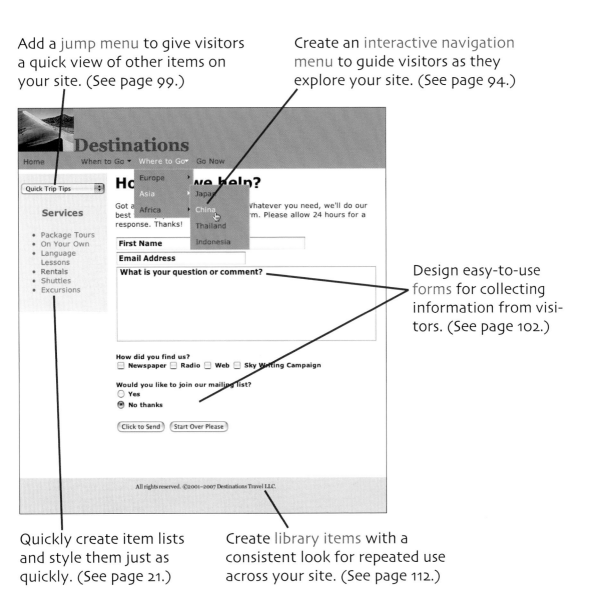

Design easy-to-use forms for collecting information from visitors. (See page 102.)

Quickly create item lists and style them just as quickly. (See page 21.)

Create library items with a consistent look for repeated use across your site. (See page 112.)

how this book works

The title explains what is covered in that section.

Names of Dreamweaver elements, file names, and other important concepts are shown in orange.

Numbered steps lead you through the sequence of actions, showing only the details you really need.

Screenshots focus on what part of Dreamweaver you'll be using for that particular project step.

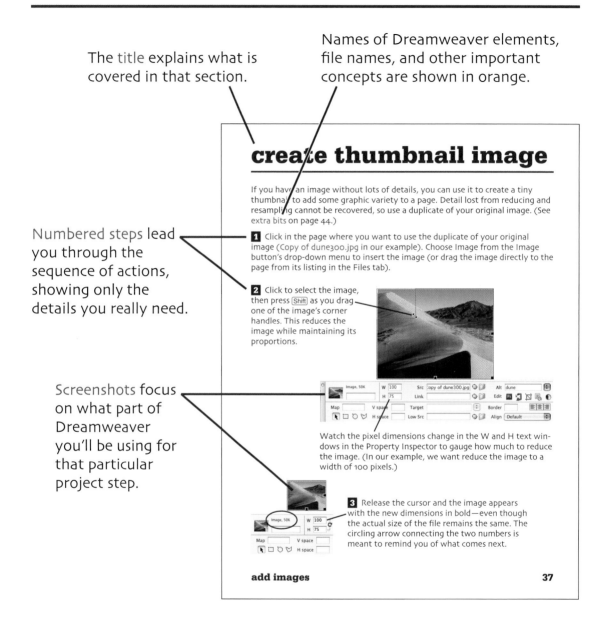

create thumbnail image

If you have an image without lots of details, you can use it to create a tiny thumbnail to add some graphic variety to a page. Detail lost from reducing and resampling cannot be recovered, so use a duplicate of your original image. (See extra bits on page 44.)

1 Click in the page where you want to use the duplicate of your original image (Copy of dune300.jpg in our example). Choose Image from the Image button's drop-down menu to insert the image (or drag the image directly to the page from its listing in the Files tab).

2 Click to select the image, then press [Shift] as you drag one of the image's corner handles. This reduces the image while maintaining its proportions.

Watch the pixel dimensions change in the W and H text windows in the Property Inspector to gauge how much to reduce the image. (In our example, we want reduce the image to a width of 100 pixels.)

3 Release the cursor and the image appears with the new dimensions in bold—even though the actual size of the file remains the same. The circling arrow connecting the two numbers is meant to remind you of what comes next.

add images 37

The extra bits section at the end of each chapter contains additional tips and tricks that you might like to know—but that aren't absolutely necessary for creating the Web page. As you work through a section, flip back to see the related extra bits rather than wait until you finish the entire chapter.

crop image

extra bits

The heading for each group of tips matches the section title. (The colors are just for decoration and have no hidden meaning.)

image tools p. 26

- Ignore the blank text window to the right of the thumbnail, which is for scripts.

add image p. 27

- Keep your site's top-level folder uncluttered by creating new sub-folders when you have more than three or four related pages. Open the Files panel and right-click (Windows) or Ctrl-click (Mac) to see the New Folder choice in the context menu.

- The root folder contains all your Web site's files. (In our example, it's dwCS3 example site.) An images subfolder within the root folder makes it easier to find your photos or graphics.

- Always add Alt text for your images. For dialup Web visitors, the alt text appears quickly, enabling them to skip the page if they don't want to wait for the full image. Alt text also is used by special audio Web browsers for visually impaired visitors. If the image is something like a horizontal rule, choose <empty> from the drop-down menu.

crop image p. 33

- In our example, we crop an image already inserted into a page/ You also can open an image directly from the Files panel, make your crops, and then insert it into a page. Choose the workflow that feels most natural, then stick with it for consistent results.

- It's easy to wind up with several different sizes of the same image for different sections of your layout. By including the image's pixel width at the end of its name, such as janustemple180.jpg, it's easy to remember which is which.

adjust brightness p. 36

- The sliders can be hard to control, so type numbers in the text windows for fine adjustments.

create thumbnail image p. 37

- You could use resampling to enlarge an image, but don't. The quality will suffer noticeably. Instead, use your regular image-editing program with the (presumably) larger original.

- When you click the Resample button, a dialog box warns you that the change is permanent. Since we're using a duplicate, click OK.

44

add images

Next to the heading there's a page number that also shows which section the tips belong to.

the web site

You can find this book's companion site at
http://www.waywest.net/dwvqj/.

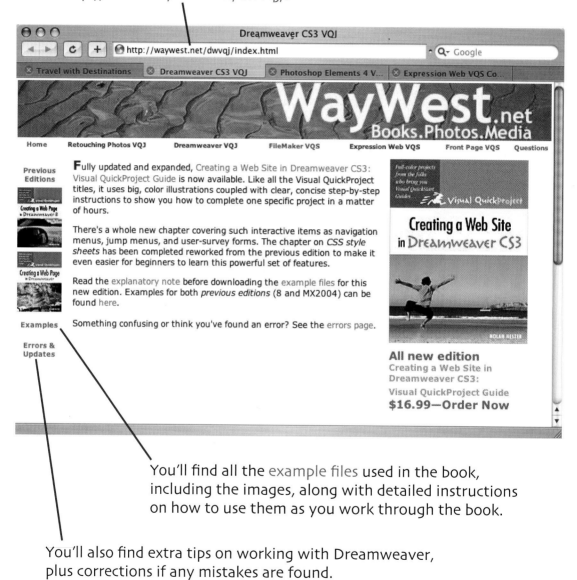

You'll find all the example files used in the book,
including the images, along with detailed instructions
on how to use them as you work through the book.

You'll also find extra tips on working with Dreamweaver,
plus corrections if any mistakes are found.

useful tools

Naturally, you'll need a computer, and you'll need Dreamweaver CS3, which is packed with most of the tools you'll need, including a way to publish to the Web.

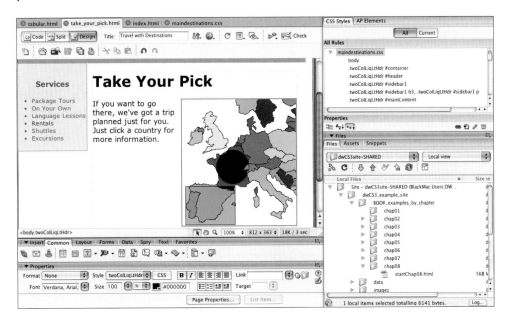

You'll also need an image editor. If you bought Dreamweaver as part of either version of the Adobe Creative Suite 3 Web Editions, then you'll be able to use Fireworks, which is a full-fledged image editor designed to work hand-in-hand with Dreamweaver. Your digital camera may have included an image-editing program. Otherwise, consider Adobe Photoshop Elements, which also contains specific tools for working with Web images.

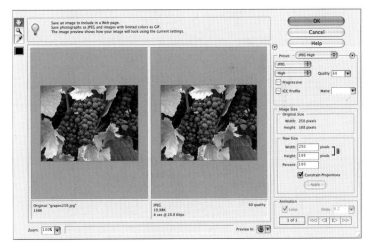

the next step

While this Visual QuickProject Guide gives you a good start on creating a Web site using Dreamweaver, there is a lot more to learn. If you want to dive into all the details, try Dreamweaver CS3 for Windows and Macintosh: Visual QuickStart Guide, by Tom Negrino and Dori Smith.

The Dreamweaver CS3: Visual Quick-Start Guide features clear examples, concise step-by-step instructions, and tons of helpful tips. With more than 500 pages, it covers darn near every aspect of Dreamweaver.

Peachpit Bestseller

VISUAL QUICKSTART GUIDE

DREAMWEAVER CS3

Learn Dreamweaver the Quick and Easy Way!

FOR WINDOWS AND MACINTOSH

TOM NEGRINO
DORI SMITH

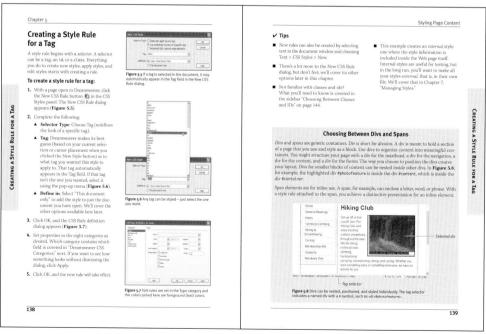

1. welcome to dreamweaver

Adobe Dreamweaver CS3 is a powerful program, packed with cool features to create Web sites. So packed, in fact, that it can be a bit overwhelming.

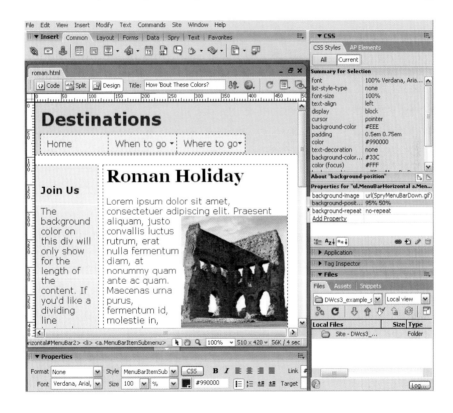

Not to worry. We aren't going to explain every possible option—just the crucial ones to keep you going, no matter how daunting Dreamweaver may seem initially. We'll have some fun along the way, too, so let's get started.

explore dreamweaver

A series of key toolbars, windows, and panels surrounds your main Dreamweaver document. Take a moment to understand how these tools work and you'll save yourself frustration later. (See extra bits on page 9.)

When you open more than one file, a series of tabs appears across the top of the main window to indicate which ones are open.

The current file's title appears at the center of the toolbar, followed by some buttons related to posting your site on the Web.

Use the high-lighted button to see a ruler or grid while building pages.

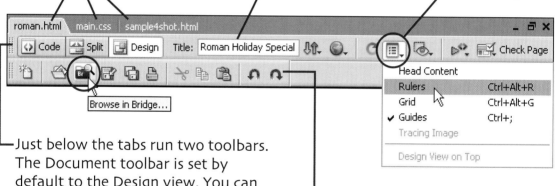

Just below the tabs run two toolbars. The Document toolbar is set by default to the Design view. You can change it to show only the Code view or use the Split view to show the Code and Design views.

Use the buttons in the Standard toolbar to create new files, open folders, cut and paste, save files, and undo actions. The highlighted button enables you to switch to Adobe Bridge, a great tool now included with Dreamweaver for quickly finding your images. (See page 6.)

Choose a tab in the Insert toolbar to display related buttons for a variety of tasks. To show or hide toolbars, including Insert, choose View > Toolbars and make a choice in the drop-down menu. (To expand or collapse the Insert toolbar, click the arrow next to Insert.)

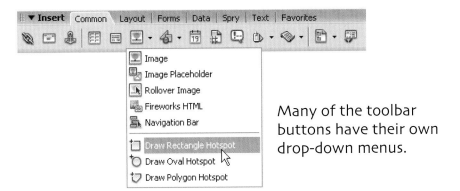

Many of the toolbar buttons have their own drop-down menus.

explore dreamweaver (cont.)

The Layout tab now includes four buttons for creating dynamic items such as drop-down menus, tabbed panels, and mouse-triggered expansion or collapse of page sections. While based on JavaScript, these Spry widgets are easy to use, making quick work of adding navigation menus to your Web pages. (See page 94.)

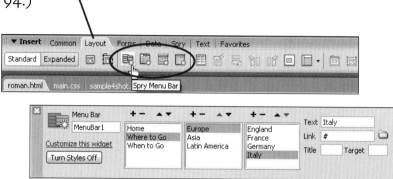

Depending on what you've selected, the Property Inspector changes to display the relevant information and tools, such as those for text or images.

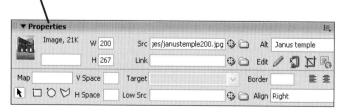

To see or hide the inspector, press Ctrl F3 (Windows) or ⌘ F3 (Mac).

The Files panel group gives you quick access to all your site's files, plus Assets and Snippets, which hold your most used images, color swatches, and bits of code. To show or hide the panel, press F8 .

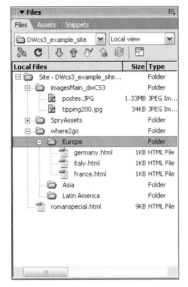

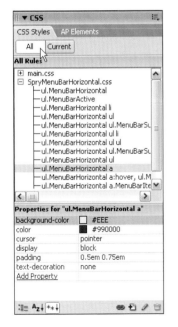

The CSS panel group helps you keep track of which styles are being used (left) or the details of a particular style (right). To show or hide the panel, press Shift F11 . For more details, see page 78. (Also see extra bits on page 9).

explore dreamweaver (cont.)

A great new feature of Dreamweaver CS3 is the inclusion of Adobe Bridge, which helps you quickly find images even if they are scattered across many folders and multiple hard drives. You can launch the program directly or by clicking the Bridge button in Dreamweaver's Standard toolbar (see page 2).

Click Bridge's upper right button to toggle between a compact and big-screen view of your image files.

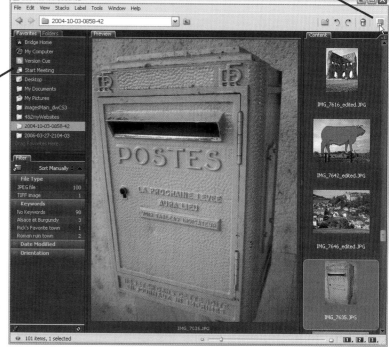

The Favorites list makes it easy to jump among your most used images. You can drag images directly from Bridge into Dreamweaver Web pages. For more information, see pages 31–32.

set up local site

Once you've installed Dreamweaver, your first step is to set up a local version of your Web site on your computer. (See extra bits on page 9.)

1 Launch Dreamweaver and when the Start Page appears, click the Dreamweaver Site button.

2 Dreamweaver automatically assigns a generic name to your new site and highlights it in the Basic tab of the Site Definition dialog box. Switch to the Advanced screen by clicking the tab.

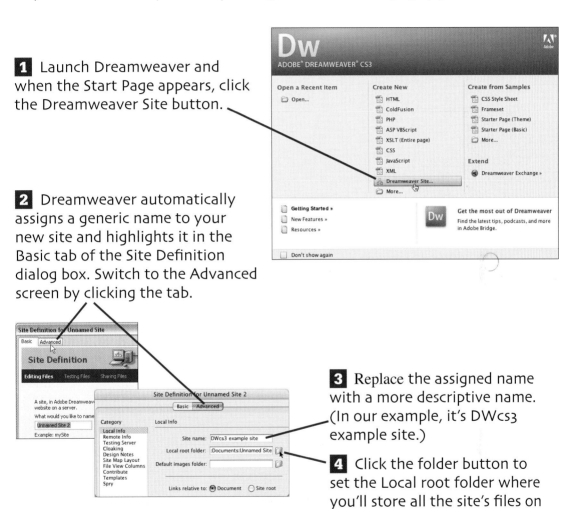

3 Replace the assigned name with a more descriptive name. (In our example, it's DWcs3 example site.)

4 Click the folder button to set the Local root folder where you'll store all the site's files on your computer.

set up local site (cont.)

5 Navigate to where you want to store the local root folder, select or create a folder, and click Select (Windows) or Choose (Mac).

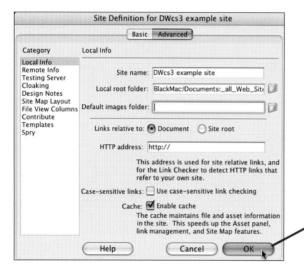

6 That's all we need to do for now, so when the Site Definition dialog box reappears, click OK to close the dialog box.

7 The local site is added to the Files pane. You're ready to start building your site, as explained in the next chapter.

welcome to dreamweaver

extra bits

explore dreamweaver p. 2

- Unless you're familiar with HTML or CSS coding, leave the toolbar set to Design.

- Rather than explain every tool and button here, we'll cover them in the coming chapters as we need them. We also don't cover items more suited to experienced users, such as the Files panel's Snippets tab, which can store frequently used bits of code.

- You also can see or hide the contents of any panel by clicking the triangle-shaped arrow at the upper left of the panel.

- When editing CSS styles, Dreamweaver lets you choose whether double-clicking a style in the CSS panel takes you to the Property Inspector or a special CSS dialog box. By default, it's set to the CSS dialog box, which I find better organized. If you want to switch to the Inspector, choose Ctrl U (Windows) or ⌘ U (Mac), then choose CSS Styles and change the setting in the bottom button group.

set up local site p. 7

- The name you enter in the Site Definition window only appears within Dreamweaver, not on your actual Web site. Pick one to distinguish this site from the many others you'll no doubt be creating soon.

- If your computer has a second hard drive, store your root folder there instead of on your main hard drive. That way if the heavily used main drive goes bad, your local site files remain safe.

2. create a basic web site

Thanks to Dreamweaver's style sheet–based layouts, it's relatively simple to create a basic Web site with pages that share the same design and navigation buttons. In this chapter, you'll start by using a basic layout to create a simple home page. In later chapters, you'll learn to dress it up a bit with images and some special features. Here, however, we'll focus on the basics: creating, naming, titling, and saving this all-important page.

Our logo

Destinations

Services

Roman Holiday

- Package Tours
- On Your Own
- Language Lessons
- Rentals
- Shuttles
- Excursions

You can have your own fabulous Roman holididay without ever setting foot in the Eternal City. Avoid the big city crush by exploring the great Roman architecture found across the rest of Europe.

You'll find plenty of history and culture—from Romania's forests to the plains of Spain and the valleys of France.

Getting Around

If you want to tool around on a little Vespa, as Audrey Hepburn did in Rome, we're ready for you. Or if a compact camper is more your style, Gregory Peck just might want to go along.

Don't let this relatively plain example page fool you. Built with Dreamweaver's predesigned page layouts using Cascading Style Sheets, it offers a solid foundation for an entire Web site. Watch it grow as we move through each chapter.

create a home page

The mechanics of creating a Web site are pretty simple. The first step is to create a new page, then name the file, give it a title, and save it. While you can give the home page any title you wish, try to use something that helps visitors immediately understand your site's purpose. If you have not already done so, launch Dreamweaver, and the site you defined in Chapter 1 opens by default. (See extra bits on page 24.)

1 Use the Menu bar to choose File > New (⌃Ctrl⌐N in Windows, ⌘N on the Mac).

2 When the New Document dialog box appears, select Blank Page on the left (HTML will be selected automatically in the middle) and then make a choice in the Layout column. In our example, we're using the two-column liquid layout with a left sidebar, header and footer. (Liquid simply means that the layout automatically adjusts to the width of the user's Web browser window—a good approach for most layouts.)

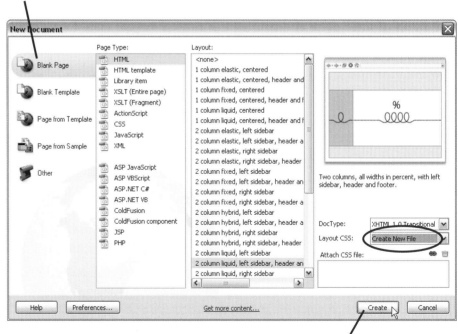

3 Below the right column's preview area, make sure the Layout CSS drop-down menu is set to Create New File before you click Create.

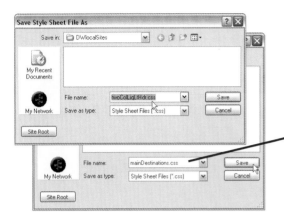

4 Dreamweaver automatically offers to save the site's style sheet in the root folder you defined in Chapter 1. But instead of applying a name based on the layout style (twoColLiqLtHdr.css in the example), name it based on your site's name (mainDestinations.css in the example). Click Save.

5 Dreamweaver saves the CSS page and adds it to the site's list of files. At the same time, it creates a new untitled Web page (html file) based on that layout.

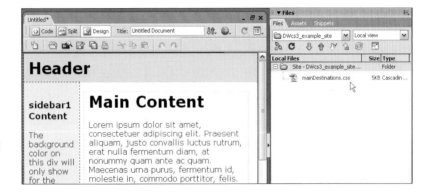

6 Click inside the page's Title text window, and type in your own title for the page. (Our sample site uses Travel with Destinations, the name of our fictitious travel company.) Visitors to your site will see the title at the top of their browser window, where it acts as a label for your site. It's not the same as the page's file name—as you'll see in the next step.

create a home page (cont.)

7 From the Menu bar, choose File > Save (⌃Ctrl⌃S in Windows, ⌘⌃S on the Mac). In the Save As dialog box that opens, navigate to the site folder you created in Chapter 1. This will be your home page, so name it index and click Save. (Dreamweaver automatically adds the .html suffix.)

8 The page's name is added to the list of site files in the Files tab. Right-click it there and choose Set as Home Page in the drop-down menu. Before going on, save your work (⌃Ctrl⌃S in Windows, ⌘⌃S on the Mac).

add text

Adding text to a Web page in Dreamweaver is not that different from using a word processing program, with the exception of using certain special characters explained in step 3. (See extra bits on page 24.)

1 Start by replacing some of the home page's placeholder material. Double-click the top header to select it, and type in your site's name. In our example, it's Destinations. Don't worry about how it looks— we'll format all this material later using style sheets.

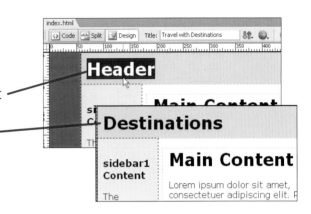

2 As you enter your text in the main column, press Enter (Windows) or Return (Mac) to start a new paragraph, just as you would with a word processing program. Type in the rest of your text, setting off each line as a separate paragraph. In our example, we've entered a description of the Roman Holiday travel package.

add text (cont.)

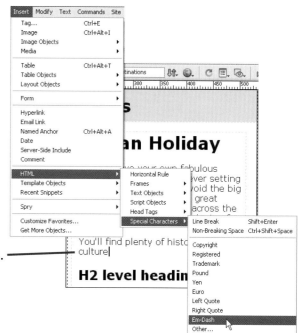

3 Unlike with word processing programs, certain characters cannot be typed directly into a Web page. In our example, we want to add an em-dash right after the word culture. Choose Insert > HTML > Special Characters, and choose Em-Dash from the drop-down menu to insert the character.

Roman Holiday

You can have your own fabulous Roman holidiay without ever setting foot in the Eternal City. Avoid the big city crush by exploring the great Roman architecture found across the rest of Europe.

You'll find plenty of history and culture—from Romania's forests to the plains of Spain and the valleys of France.

H2 level heading

4 Once the em-dash is inserted, we can add the rest of the text.

5 Save your changes (Ctrl S in Windows, ⌘S on the Mac).

create a basic web site

insert image placeholder

In a perfect world, all your images would be ready to put into your Web pages right when you're building them. In reality, someone else may be creating the image even though you need to get started building pages. That's why I explain inserting an image placeholder right in the middle of this text-building chapter. You always can add the image later (as explained in Chapter 3), but this trick lets you keep working.

1 If you closed your home page previously, reopen it. Click in the header just before its title (Destinations, in our example) and then click the Split view button.

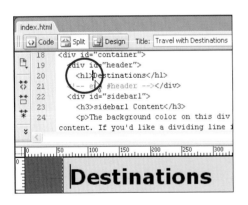 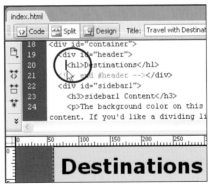

2 We want to insert our company logo here but, as the Split view shows, there's a slight problem. The cursor is sitting after the opening <h1> header tag. Fix the problem by repositioning your cursor just before the <h1> tag.

insert placeholder (cont.)

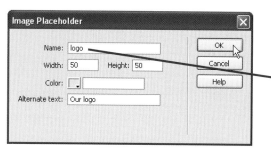

3 From the Menu bar, choose Insert > Image Objects > Image Placeholder. Type in a memory-jogging name for the image-to-come (logo, in our example). If you know the image's exact width and height in pixels, type it in. Otherwise, enter an approximate size. Finally, enter Alternate text that briefly describes the image or its function. Click OK to close the dialog box and press F5 to refresh the Design view.

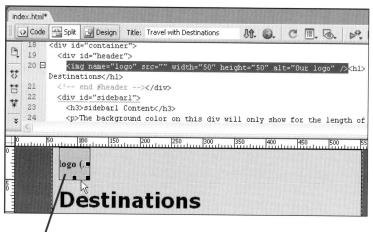

4 Dreamweaver inserts a box into the Web page based on your chosen width and height, helping you gauge how the page will look—and, most importantly, reminding you that you're still missing an image. Close the Split view by clicking the Design button, and save your changes (Ctrl S in Windows, ⌘ S on the Mac).

create a basic web site

create headings

Just like newspaper and magazine headlines, headings on a Web page are larger and more noticeable than regular text. They range from size 1 (the largest) to size 6 (the smallest). Whether you're building your own page or using our example page, the basics of creating and changing headings remain the same. Just like a newspaper, larger sizes generally are used for more important items and smaller sizes for less important items. (See extra bits on page 24.)

1 If you closed your home page previously, reopen it. Make sure that you're working in Design view and that the Property Inspector is visible (⌊Ctrl⌋⌊F3⌋ in Windows, ⌘⌊F3⌋ on the Mac).

2 Double-click the first heading in the example page's main column (Roman Holiday) to select it. The Property Inspector lists its Format as Heading 1. Another clue about the heading's format can be found in the bottom status bar, where the last tag listed is <h1>.

3 Click anywhere in the same column's second heading (H2 level heading), and then click the <h2> tag in the status bar to select the entire head. As you'd expect, the Property Inspector lists its format as Heading 2.

create a basic web site

create headings (cont.)

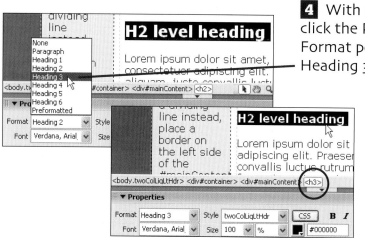

4 With the heading still selected, click the Property Inspector's Format pop-up menu and select Heading 3. The heading shrinks to reflect the new, smaller size, and the tag in the status bar changes to <h3>.

5 Now replace the heading's text by typing in your own (Getting Around in our example). We'll also replace the text below the heading with related text.

> **Getting Around**
>
> If you want to tool around on a little Vespa, as Audrey Hepburn did in Rome, we're ready for you. Or if a compact camper is more your style, Gregory Peck just might want to go along.
>
> er> <div#mainContent> <p>   100% ▾ 672 x 365

6 While we're at it, let's change the sidebar header to a Heading 4, which will look better with the main column heads. In our example, we've also renamed it Services. Don't mess with any of the other settings, such as Font or Style, which we'll fix in a later chapter using Cascading Style Sheets. Save your changes by choosing File > Save (Ctrl S in Windows, ⌘ S on the Mac).

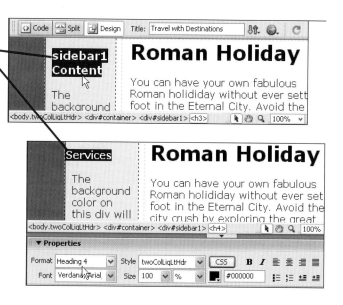

create a basic web site

create lists

Organizing information into lists, whether numbered or simply marked with bullets, makes it easy to group lots of items in a way that anyone can instantly recognize. Ordered lists are great when you need to highlight a specific sequence of steps or materials. We'll quickly show you how to do ordered and unordered lists. I'll cover the rest of the list styling, however, in the Create Styles and Layouts with CSS chapter.

1 Return to your home page and, if it's not already visible, open the Property Inspector (Window > Properties) and select everything below the heading in the sidebar.

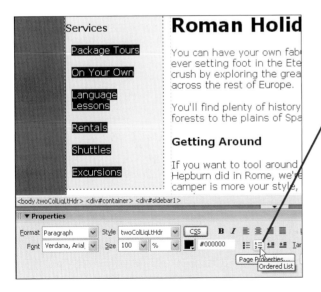

2 Type in your sidebar items, separating each with a paragraph return. Our example lists services available from the travel agency. Select all the items, and click the Ordered List button in the Property Inspector. The selected lines will be numbered in sequence from 1 to 6 below the Services heading.

create lists (cont.)

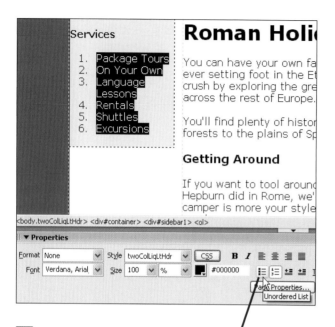

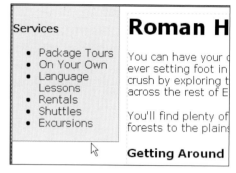

3 Reselect the items, and click the Unordered List button in the Property Inspector. The items now have small bullets instead, which in our example more clearly indicates that these are examples of available services. Save your changes (⌃Ctrl S in Windows, ⌘S on the Mac).

add a footer

Tucked at the bottom of pages, footers offer a perfect place for displaying essential information that doesn't need to immediately grab a reader's attention. Copyright and contact information are good examples. Thanks to our example's CSS-based layout, the home page already contains a footer. For now, we'll keep it simple, though later on we'll use CSS to add some fancier formatting and navigation links.

1 Scroll to the bottom of the example page and select the layout's placeholder text.

2 Replace it by typing in your own text. In our example, that includes the formal name of the business, plus copyright information. (You'll find the © by choosing Insert > HTML > Special Characters.) When you're done, click the Align Center button in the Property Inspector to put the text across the bottom-middle of the page. Be sure to save your changes ([Ctrl][S] in Windows, ⌘[S] on the Mac).

extra bits

create a home page p. 12

- While this layout is used throughout the book, feel free to choose another of the many predesigned layouts found under the Blank Page-HTML choice. The principles explained in each chapter can be applied to any of these layouts.

- Using style sheet–based layouts is the most flexible way to build your site pages. Frames-based layouts are hard to update, difficult to bookmark, and rightly fading in popularity. Layer-based layouts should be avoided as well.

- Naming your CSS file after its related Web site helps reduce confusion if you create more sites (and related CSS files) later on. By the way, don't name the style sheet based on your site's current layout because you'll inevitably tweak the configuration and won't want to keep updating the name.

- The page's file name and title serve different purposes. The file name is used behind the scenes to help you and Dreamweaver keep track of how your files are organized. For example, home pages should always be named index, which helps Web servers know that this page is the "front door" to your site. The page title is what the viewer's Web browser displays when your page is onscreen.

add text p. 15

- Macintosh computers display Web page text at about three-fourths the size that it appears on a Windows machine, so if you are building your Web site on a Windows PC, avoid the two smallest text sizes.

- To see all 99 special characters that are available, choose Insert > HTML > Special Characters > Other.

- To reach the special characters more easily, you can switch the Insert bar tab from Common to Text, then click the far-right button and choose from the drop-down menu.

create headings p. 19

- To keep your pages uncluttered, limit yourself to no more than two or three heading sizes on the same page.

create a basic web site

3. add images

While text and headlines lend structure and meaning to Web pages, it's images that give your pages real impact.

Dreamweaver can handle basic image editing; for more demanding tasks use a dedicated graphics program. Two obvious options are Adobe's own Photoshop and Fireworks programs, available individually or included in some versions of the Dreamweaver CS3 suite. With Photoshop, you can drag images directly into Dreamweaver. For other options, take a look in the graphics section of www.versiontracker.com, where you can compare prices, features, and user comments.

image tools

Use the Property Inspector as your main tool for most image work. (See extra bits on page 44.) While you can use the Edit buttons to optimize or resample an image, that work is best done with a dedicated graphics program (such as Fireworks or Photoshop) before you begin laying out your Web pages.

Displayed near the image thumbnail is the file size (20K in our example) and its W (width) and H (height) in pixels.

Src tells you where the image is stored, while Link tells you what file (if any) the image is linked to if clicked.

Alt lets you create a label to be read aloud by browsers created for visually handicapped visitors. Also use Alt to describe an image for visitors who have turned off image downloading for speedier surfing.

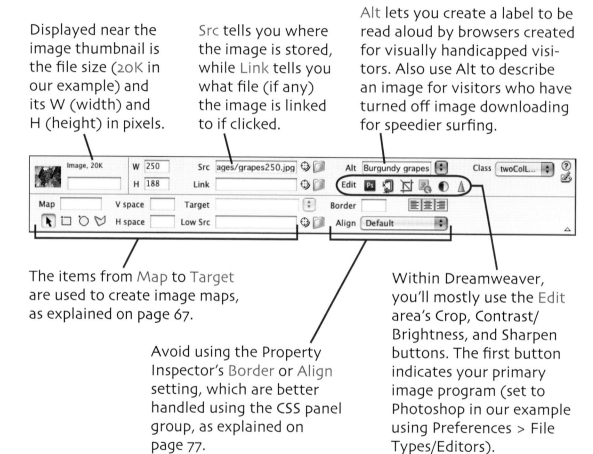

The items from Map to Target are used to create image maps, as explained on page 67.

Avoid using the Property Inspector's Border or Align setting, which are better handled using the CSS panel group, as explained on page 77.

Within Dreamweaver, you'll mostly use the Edit area's Crop, Contrast/ Brightness, and Sharpen buttons. The first button indicates your primary image program (set to Photoshop in our example using Preferences > File Types/Editors).

add image

After sizing and then optimizing images in an external graphics program, you're ready to add the Web-ready versions to your Web pages. (See extra bits on page 44.)

1 Open the page in which you want to add an image. (In our example, we're once again using index.html, the home page created in the previous chapter.)

2 Make sure the Insert toolbar's Common tab is selected, and position your cursor at the beginning of the main text.

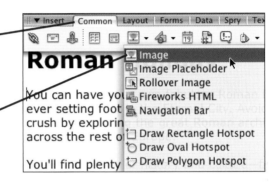

3 Choose Image from the Image button's drop-down menu.

4 When the Select Image Source dialog box appears, navigate to the image you want to use, and click Choose. (In our example, we're using janustemple200.jpg.)

add image (cont.)

5 If the image isn't already a part of your Web site, Dreamweaver asks if you want to save it in the site's root folder. Choose Yes, navigate to your site's images folder, and save the image there.

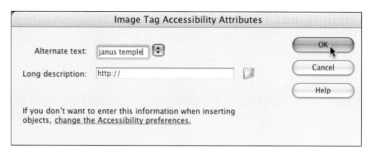

Type a brief description of the image in the Alternate text box when the dialog box appears and click OK.

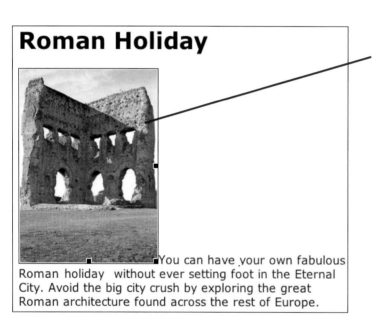

6 When the image appears on the page, save your work ([Ctrl][S] in Windows, [⌘][S] on the Mac).

add flash video

If you've used Adobe Flash to create a video, it's easy to drop it right into your page. Or, as explained on on page 31, you can add other formats, such as QuickTime, that will use plug-ins built into the viewer's Web browser.

1 Make sure the Insert toolbar's Common tab is selected. Click in the page where you want to insert a Flash video. (In our example, we're using FlashExample.html, a mostly blank duplicate of index.html.)

2 Choose Flash Video from the Plugin button's drop-down menu. Use the dialog box to navigate to the image you want to use, and click Choose. Click Yes when asked if you want to save the video in your site's root folder.

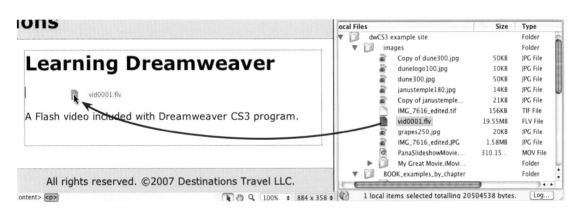

3 Once the video's in your site folder, you can click and drag it from the Files tab directly onto the page. Release your cursor.

add flash video (cont.)

4 Leave the Video type set to Progressive Download Video and use the pop-up menu to choose a Skin style for the control buttons that will appear with the video. (In our example, we're using Clear Skin 1, the least obtrusive choice.) Click the Detect Size button once to see the video's natural width and height, then type in a smaller width and height to fit your Web page. Click OK when you're done.

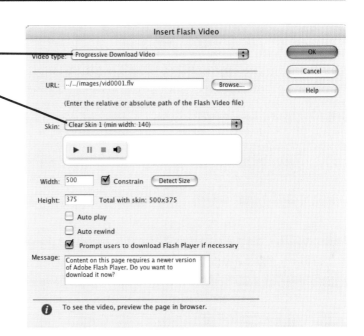

5 Dreamweaver inserts a placeholder on the page. Click the Globe button to preview the results in various Web browsers.

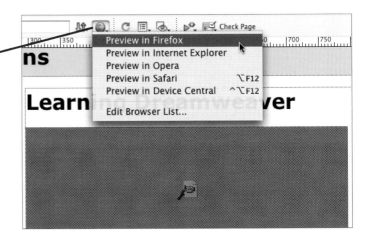

add images

add quicktime video

The process for adding a QuickTime video, or any video or audio file, is similar to the previous steps for Flash: Choose Plugin from the Plugin button's drop-down menu, navigate to the image you want to use and select it. Using Adobe Bridge, however, makes the whole thing even easier.

1 Make sure the Insert toolbar's Common tab is selected and that you've opened the page where you want to insert a QuickTime video. (In our example, we're using MovieExample.html, a mostly blank duplicate of index.html.)

2 Launch Bridge by clicking its button in the Standard toolbar (View > Toolbars > Standard).

3 In Bridge, browse until you find the QuickTime or other audio/video file you want to use. With Bridge's Preview panel open, you can play the file just by selecting the image in the Content panel.

4 Once you find the image, click the Compact View button.

add quicktime video (cont.)

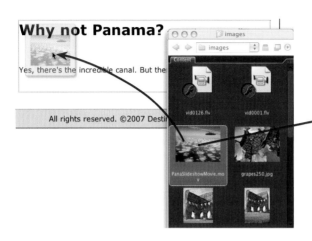

5 By default, Bridge collapses to a smaller window that floats atop all other programs, including Dreamweaver. Drag the Bridge window over to your Web page, then click and drag the thumbnail image to where you want the audio/video file to appear. Release your cursor.

6 Dreamweaver adds a placeholder to the page, and the Property Inspector Src window automatically displays the file's name and location.

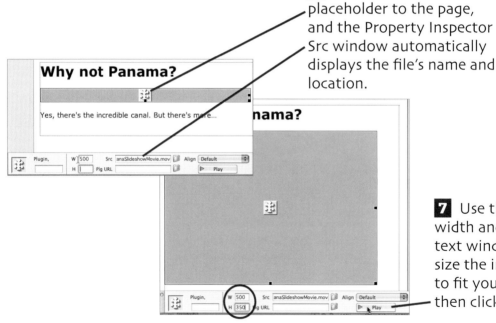

7 Use the width and height text windows to size the image to fit your page, then click Play.

8 The video plays right on your page in Dreamweaver. Click Stop in the Property Inspector when you're ready and save your work (Ctrl S in Windows, ⌘ S on the Mac).

add images

crop image

You don't need a separate graphics program for cropping images—just don't use your original image unless you create a backup duplicate. Cropping permanently alters your image, so if you make a mistake, immediately choose Undo Crop in the Edit menu. (See extra bits on page 44.)

1 In the Files tab, select the still image you previously used on page 27 (janustemple200.jpg in our example). Make a copy of it (Ctrl D in Windows, ⌘D on the Mac). Dreamweaver automatically adds a duplicate to the tab's list and names it Copy of the file name.

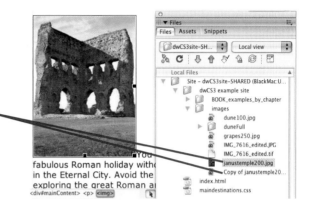

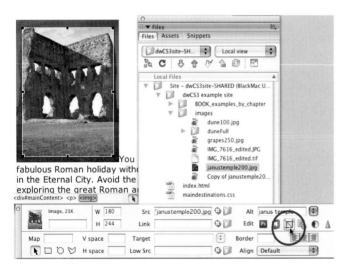

2 Reselect the original image in the Web page and click the Crop button in the Property Inspector. A selection area, marked by a line and darker surrounding area, appears in the middle of the image.

crop image (cont.)

3 Click and drag any of the black handles along the selection's edge to set your crop lines or click-and-drag in the middle to reposition the entire crop.

Double-click inside the selection and the image is trimmed.

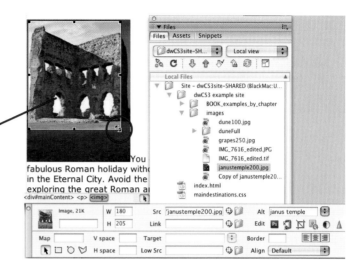

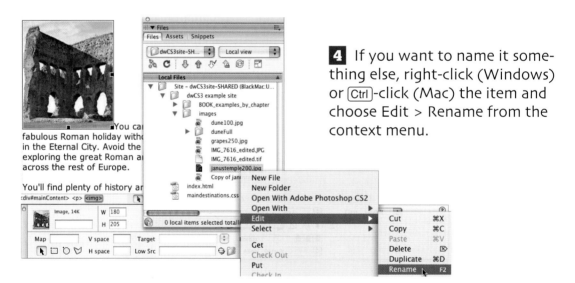

4 If you want to name it something else, right-click (Windows) or Ctrl-click (Mac) the item and choose Edit > Rename from the context menu.

5 Once the name is highlighted, type in a new name and press [Enter] (Windows) or [Return] (Mac). (In our example, we use janustemple180.jpg to reflect its new cropped width of 180 pixels.) Dreamweaver needs to update the links to the page to reflect the new name, so click Update.

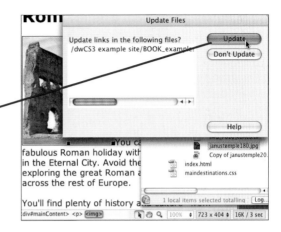

6 The Property Inspector's Src box now reflects the new name, janustemple180.jpg. Save your work ([Ctrl][S] in Windows, [⌘][S] on the Mac).

adjust brightness

A single button in the Property Inspector lets you adjust an image's brightness or contrast. Sometimes minor adjustments of either can really help a so-so image. You do not need to make a duplicate of the image. (See extra bits on page 44.)

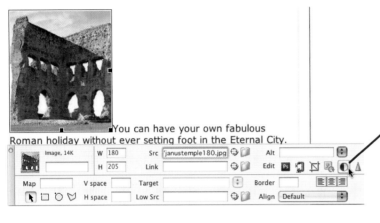

1 On your page, click to select the image that you want to adjust (janustemple180.jpg in our example). Click the Contrast/Brightness button in the Property Inspector.

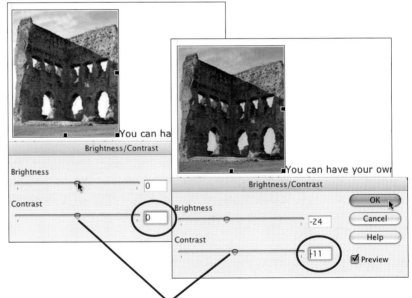

2 To change the brightness or contrast drag the sliders or enter new values in the adjacent text windows. (Increase the effects by sliding to the right or entering a larger number.) Click OK to apply your adjustments. Save your work ([Ctrl][S] in Windows, [⌘][S] on the Mac).

create thumbnail image

If you have an image without lots of details, you can use it to create a tiny thumbnail to add some graphic variety to a page. Detail lost from reducing and resampling cannot be recovered, so use a duplicate of your original image. (See extra bits on page 44.)

1 Click in the page where you want to use the duplicate of your original image (Copy of dune300.jpg in our example). Choose Image from the Image button's drop-down menu to insert the image (or drag the image directly to the page from its listing in the Files tab).

2 Click to select the image, then press [Shift] as you drag one of the image's corner handles. This reduces the image while maintaining its proportions.

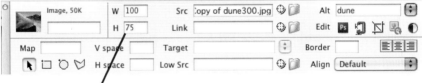

Watch the pixel dimensions change in the W and H text windows in the Property Inspector to gauge how much to reduce the image. (In our example, we want reduce the image to a width of 100 pixels.)

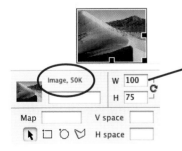

3 Release the cursor and the image appears with the new dimensions in bold—even though the actual size of the file remains the same. The circling arrow connecting the two numbers is meant to remind you of what comes next.

create thumbnail (cont.)

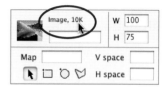

4 Click the Property Inspector's Resample button to reduce the actual file size, indicated afterward by a smaller K size in the Property Inspector.

5 Greatly reduced images often lose some crispness, so click the Property Inspector's Sharpen button.

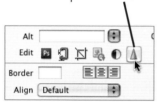

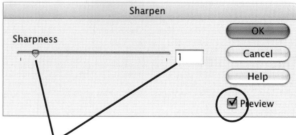

6 Be sure Preview is checked, then use the slider or text window in the Sharpen dialog box to adjust the amount. (Drag the slider to the right or enter a higher number in the text window to increase the sharpening.) Click OK when you're satisfied. Save the page before continuing.

add images

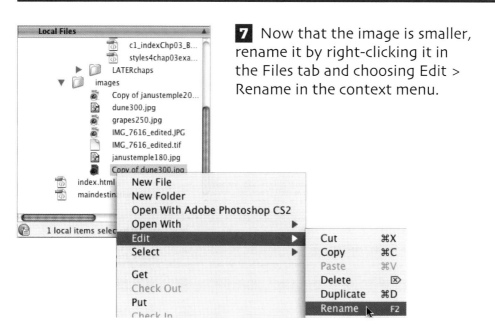

7 Now that the image is smaller, rename it by right-clicking it in the Files tab and choosing Edit > Rename in the context menu.

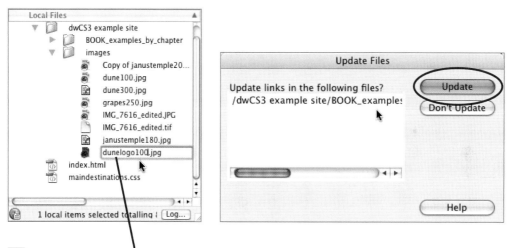

8 Type in a new name while preserving the .jpg suffix. (Our example uses dunelogo100.jpg to reflect the image's new width.) Press [Enter] (Windows) or [Return] (Mac) to apply the change. Click Update when Dreamweaver asks to update links to the renamed image.

replace placeholder

We'll use this process to replace the image placeholder created on page 17 in Chapter 2. It's similar to inserting an image except that the placeholder's Alt text is preserved.

1 Click to select the image placeholder you inserted in Chapter 2 (logo in our example).

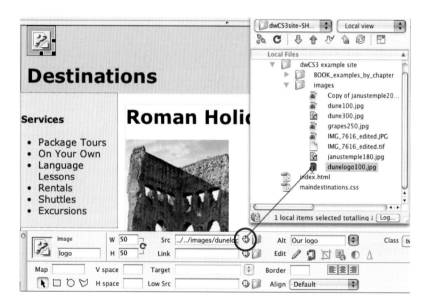

2 In the Property Inspector, click the compass-like Point to File button. Drag the line that appears to the image that will replace the placeholder (dunelogo100.jpg in our example), and release the cursor.

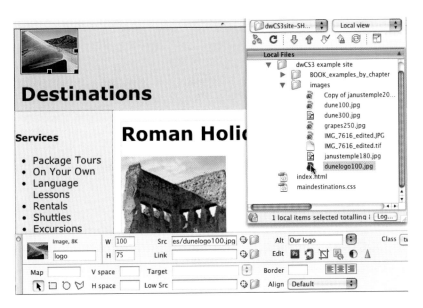

3 The new image instantly replaces the placeholder. Now that we've replaced the logo with the thumbnail, we can delete its first use lower on the example page. (We needed a place to create the thumbnail and it was simpler to do that separately from the logo-replacement process.)

4 Scroll down the page to where the first thumbnail was created and click to select it. Press ⌫Backspace (Windows) or Delete (Mac) to remove the image. Save your work (Ctrl S in Windows, ⌘ S on the Mac).

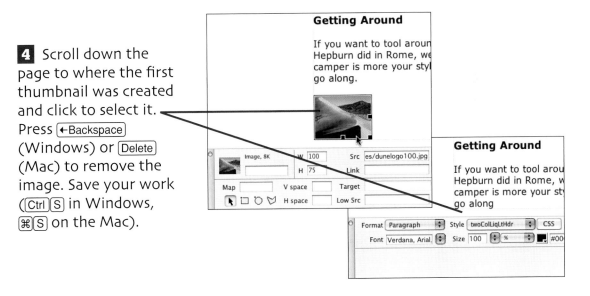

flow text around images

Wrapping blocks of text around your images creates a tighter, more professional page layout. In previous versions of Dreamweaver, the Property Inspector was the tool used most often to wrap text around images. Using the CSS Styles tab instead gives you more control, and makes it easier to update those styles as needed. Don't worry, we're simply going to apply some existing CSS rules to get our feet wet. The big CSS plunge comes in Chapter 6.

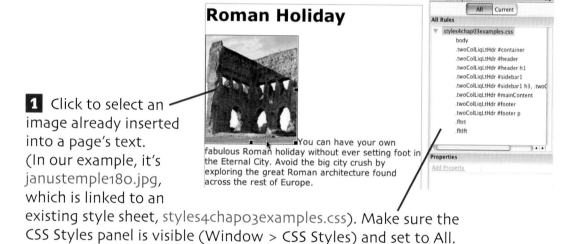

1 Click to select an image already inserted into a page's text. (In our example, it's janustemple18o.jpg, which is linked to an existing style sheet, styles4chap03examples.css). Make sure the CSS Styles panel is visible (Window > CSS Styles) and set to All.

2 Near the bottom of the list of CSS rules, right-click the rule called .fltrt and choose Apply from the context menu.

3 The selected image floats to the right side of the page with a bit of space separating it from the words now on the left. That's because the .fltrt rule has two properties: a right float and a left margin of 8px (pixels).

4 Insert another image farther down the page (grapes250.jpg from the images folder in our example). In the CSS Styles list, right-click the rule called .fltlft and select Apply from the context menu.

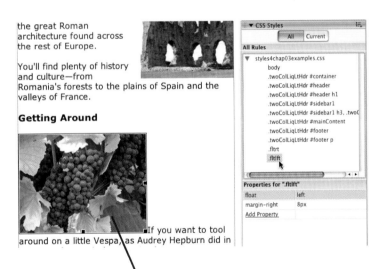

The image floats to the left with the same 8-pixel margin down the right side, exactly the properties listed for the .fltlft rule. Save your work ([Ctrl][S] in Windows, [⌘][S] on the Mac).

extra bits

image tools p. 26

- Ignore the blank text window to the right of the thumbnail, which is for scripts.

add image p. 27

- Keep your site's top-level folder uncluttered by creating new sub-folders when you have more than three or four related pages. Open the Files panel and right-click (Windows) or Ctrl-click (Mac) to see the New Folder choice in the context menu.

- The root folder contains all your Web site's files. (In our example, it's dwCS3 example site.) An images subfolder within the root folder makes it easier to find your photos or graphics.

- Always add Alt text for your images. For dialup Web visitors, the alt text appears quickly, enabling them to skip the page if they don't want to wait for the full image. Special audio Web browsers also use Alt text for visually impaired visitors. If the image is something like a horizontal rule, choose <empty> from the drop-down menu.

crop image p. 33

- In our example, we crop an image already inserted into a page. You also can open an image directly from the Files panel, make your crops, and then insert it into a page. Choose the workflow that feels most natural, then stick with it for consistent results.

- It's easy to wind up with several different sizes of the same image for different sections of your layout. By including the image's pixel width at the end of its name, such as janustemple180.jpg, it's easy to remember which is which.

adjust brightness p. 36

- The sliders can be hard to control, so type numbers in the text windows for fine adjustments.

create thumbnail image p. 37

- You could use resampling to enlarge an image, but don't. The quality will suffer noticeably. Instead, use your regular image-editing program with the (presumably) larger original.

- When you click the Resample button, a dialog box warns you that the change is permanent. Since we're using a duplicate, click OK.

add images

4. add tables

While it once was common to use tables to create layouts, Cascading Style Sheets thankfully now offer a more powerful and flexible approach. For that reason, this chapter focuses on columnar tables.

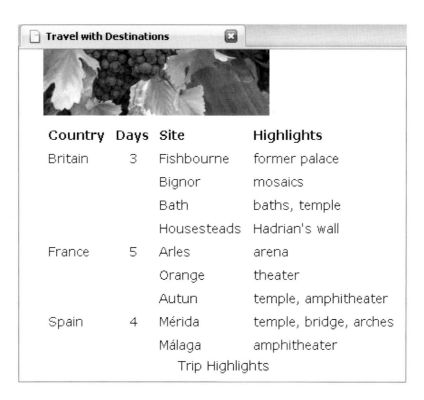

Country	Days	Site	Highlights
Britain	3	Fishbourne	former palace
		Bignor	mosaics
		Bath	baths, temple
		Housesteads	Hadrian's wall
France	5	Arles	arena
		Orange	theater
		Autun	temple, amphitheater
Spain	4	Mérida	temple, bridge, arches
		Málaga	amphitheater

Trip Highlights

add a table

Tables provide a great way to corral information into easy-to-scan rows and columns. (See extra bits on page 57.)

1 Open the page in which you want to add a table. (In our example, we're once again using index.html, the home page used in the previous chapter.) Make sure that the Property Inspector is visible, and that the Insert toolbar's Common tab is selected.

2 Press ⌅Enter (Windows) or ⌅Return (Mac) to start a fresh paragraph. Click the Table button in the Common tab.

style, Gregory Peck just might want to go along.

3 When the Table dialog box appears, use the text boxes to set the Table width and whether you want to include a Header, which creates bold-faced labels for the darkened cells. (In our example, we've set Rows to 3, Columns to 3, Table width to 400 pixels, Border thickness to 0 and Cell padding to 3 pixels.) Click OK to insert the new table.

Use the Accessibility section to create and align a caption that's used by audio-based Web browsers.

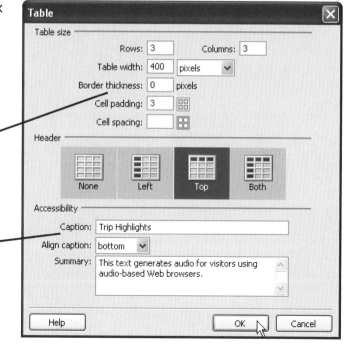

4 When the new table appears, type your labels into the header cells, where they are boldfaced. Type the rest of your table content into each cell, pressing Tab to move from cell to cell. Don't bother formatting the text; do it after you read Chapter 6 and it'll be a snap.

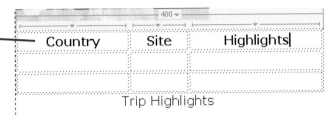

5 If you need more cells as you type, switch the Insert toolbar to the Layout tab.

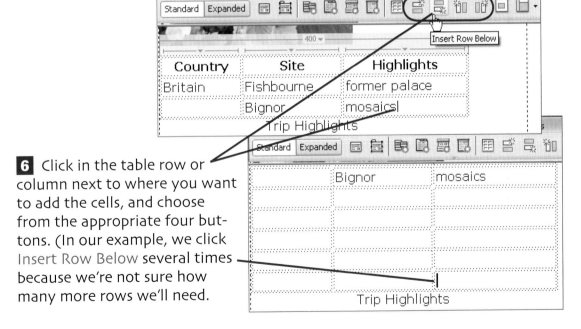

6 Click in the table row or column next to where you want to add the cells, and choose from the appropriate four buttons. (In our example, we click Insert Row Below several times because we're not sure how many more rows we'll need.

7 Finish typing your information into the table. Save your work (Ctrl S in Windows, ⌘ S on the Mac).

select, change table parts

Inevitably as you create tables, you'll need to tweak them in various ways, whether it's removing extra rows, adding a column, or moving the whole table. This section covers the changes you'll make most often. For more elaborate formatting options, see Chapter 6. (See extra bits on page 57.)

1 If you've closed it, reopen the page where you added a table in the previous steps and, if necessary, add an extra row using the Insert Row Below button. (Our example table in index.html already has an extra row at the bottom.)

Country	Site	Highlights
Britain	Fishbourne	former palace
	Bignor	mosaics
France	Arles	arena
	Orange	theater
	Autun	temple, amphitheater
Spain	Mérida	temple, bridge, arches
	Málaga	amphitheater

2 Ordinarily you select a row by moving your cursor to the table's left side whereupon it becomes a big, bold arrow. However, as in our example, a table often sits flush left, making that method difficult. It's easier to use the status bar's tag selector: Click in any cell in that extra row and the cell's tag <td> is highlighted in the status bar.

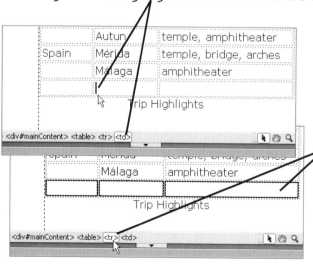

3 Just to the left of the cell's tag is the row's tag <tr>. Click it and the entire row is selected.

4 Press ←Backspace (Windows) or Delete (Mac) and the selected row is removed.

5 To add a new column, move your cursor to the top of a column running down either side of where you want it to go. The cursor becomes a bold arrow.

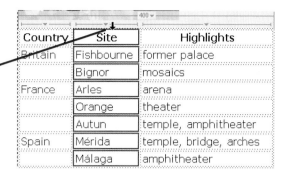

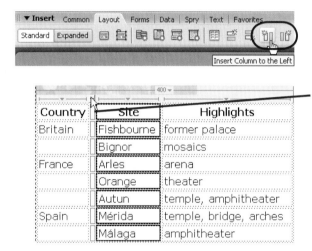

6 In the Layout tab of the Insert toolbar, click one of the two Insert Column buttons to insert to the left or right of the selected column. A new blank column is inserted in the table.

7 Use the status bar's magnify pop-up menu to zoom in a bit on the column so you can add your information.

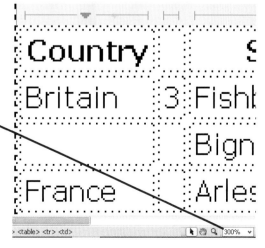

change table parts (cont.)

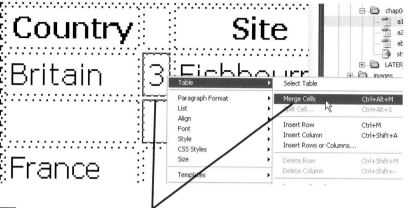

8 If you want to merge several cells into one, drag the cursor across the multiple cells (in our example the 3 and the blank cell below it). Right-click, choose Table > Merge Cells from the context menu, and the cells are merged.

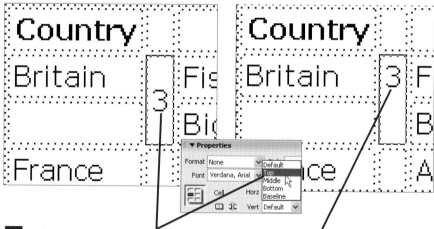

9 After merging cells, you may need to change the content's vertical alignment (in our example the 3 is centered vertically when we want it at the top). With the cells selected, click the Property Inspector's Vert pop-up menu, choose a new setting, and it's applied to the content. Repeat the steps for any other cells you've merged.

10 Remember to type in a header/label for any new columns. It's automatically boldfaced.

add tables

11 If you need to adjust the horizontal alignment of a column's text, select the cells, click the Property Inspector's Horz pop-up menu, choose a new setting, and it's applied to the content.

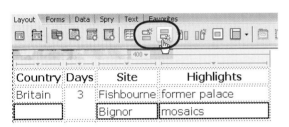

12 To add a row, select the row above or below as explained in steps 2 and 3. In the Layout tab of the Insert toolbar, click one of the two Insert Row buttons, and a new blank row is inserted in the table.

13 Save your work (Ctrl S in Windows, ⌘ S on the Mac), and click the Document toolbar's Globe button to preview the results in various Web browsers.

import tabular data

Nothing beats a table for clearly presenting spreadsheet data or tab-separated text imported from a word-processing document. More importantly, in a world full of tab-delimited data such as Excel spreadsheets, importing such text can save you hours of typing. (See extra bits on page 57.)

1 Open a page into which you want to place tabular data from another program. (In our example, we've duplicated index.html from the previous section and deleted everything in the main content area. After renaming it tabular.html, we've saved it to our example site.)

2 Click in the page where you want the data placed.

Roman Holiday: Details

3 In the Data tab of the Insert toolbar, click the first button to import your tabular data.

add tables

4 Click Browse to navigate to where you've stored the spreadsheet or word-processing document.

5 For the Delimiter, use Tab (or whatever format you used when saving the document you're now importing). In the Table width section, choose Set to and use the adjacent text windows to specify that width (90 percent in our example). Skip the padding and spacing settings, set the Format top row to [No Formatting] and click OK.

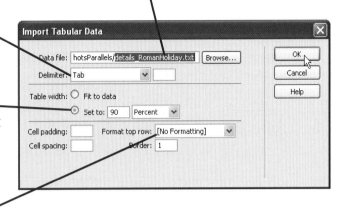

6 The data appears on the Web page arranged in its own table. Inevitably, our example table has a few errors. The same methods covered in the previous section work for the imported table, so clean up as needed.

Roman Holiday: Details

90% (427)

Roman Holiday Tour Fall 2008			
Be aware that details of this itinerary may change as circumstances dictate. We make every effort to keep this up to date. For updates, visit our Web site.			
Country	Location & Sites	Days	Comments
Britain	Pickup at Heathrow, first night in London	1	Those not battling jet lag will spend evening in West End
	Train to Fishbourne for lunch, 1st villa	1	

import tabular data (cont.)

7 In general, resist the urge to apply a lot of formatting to the imported table since that's best done using style sheets, as explained in Chapter 6. However, in our example, we're using the Property Inspector to apply the Heading 4 format to the table's header. In Chapter 6, we'll further define the Heading 4 using CSS, and that style will automatically update this page.

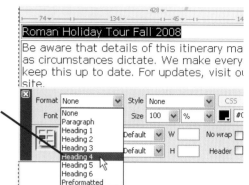

8 Save your work page (Ctrl S in Windows, ⌘ S on the Mac), and click the Document toolbar's Globe button to preview the results in various Web browsers.

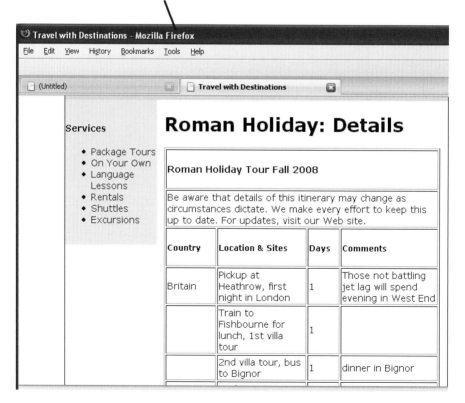

sort tables

Dreamweaver can automatically sort tabular data by column—a neat trick that lets you tinker with how the data is organized long after you've imported it into your table. There's just one catch: tables cannot be sorted if they include any cells spanning multiple columns, such as the merged cells in our current example. With a quick cut and paste, however, it's easy to work around this restriction as long as the merged cells are not scattered through the table. (See extra bits on page 57.)

1 Select the part of your table without any merged cells. (In our example, it's everything below the "Be aware" note.) Cut it from the page ([Ctrl][X] in Windows, ⌘[X] on the Mac).

Roman Holiday: Details

Roman Holiday Tour Fall 2008
Be aware that details of this itinerary may change as circumstances dictate. We make every effort to keep this up to date. For updates, visit our Web site.

2 Once the section is cut, click just below the remaining part of the table and repaste the deleted portion ([Ctrl][V] in Windows, ⌘[V] on the Mac).

The material reappears as a separate table, which you can now sort.

Use the status bar's tag selector to click the `<table>` tag, then choose Commands > Sort Table to open the Sort Table dialog box.

Roman Holiday Tour Fall 2008			
Be aware that details of this itinerary may change as circumstances dictate. We make every effort to keep this up to date. For updates, visit our Web site.			
Country	Location & Sites	Days	Comments
Britain	Pickup at Heathrow, first night in London	1	Those not battling jet lag will spend evening in West End
	Train to Fishbourne for lunch, 1st villa tour	1	
	2nd villa tour, bus to Bignor	1	dinner in Bignor
	am lecture on Roman mosaics		
	Bath	2	
	Train to Housesteads	1	Hadrian's wall, night train to Heathrow
France			

Roman Holiday Tour Fall 2008			
Be aware that details of this itinerary may change as circumstances dictate. We make every effort to keep this up to date. For updates, visit our Web			
Country	Location & Sites	Days	Comments
Britain	Pickup at Heathrow, first night in London	1	Those not battling jet lag will spend evening in West End
	Train to Fishbourne for lunch, 1st villa tour	1	
	2nd villa tour, bus to Bignor	1	dinner in Bignor
	am lecture on Roman mosaics		

sort tables (cont.)

3 Use the Sort by drop-down menu to choose which column controls the sort, then use the Order drop-down menu to set whether the sort is done Alphabetically (or Numerically) and whether it's in Ascending (or Descending) order. In our example, we sort by Column 3 (Days). We also set Then by to sort using Column 1 (Country). Click Apply to preview the sort.

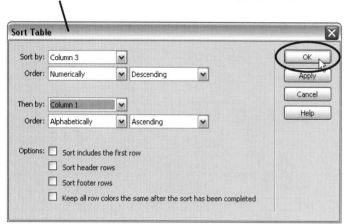

4 Dreamweaver sorts the table based on your choices. Adjust the Sort Table choices if necessary and click Apply once again. When you're satisfied, click OK to close the dialog box.

Country	Location & Sites	Days	Comments
Total Days		6	
	Bath	2	
	2nd villa tour, bus to Bignor	1	dinner in Bignor
	Train to Housesteads	1	Hadrian's wall, night train to Heathrow
	Train to		

extra bits

add a table p. 46

- The first time you use the Table dialog box it's set for three rows and columns. After that it displays the settings used for the last table you created.

- Setting the border thickness at 1 or 2 pixels (or 0 as in our example) creates a cleaner, more open look.

- Use the Table dialog box's Accessibility section to create an explanatory Caption that is read aloud by special audio Web browsers for visually impaired visitors. If needed, add details in the Summary field.

- Table cells can hold images, as well as text: The steps for inserting images into a cell are the same as those on page 27.

select, change table parts p. 48

- If you're having trouble selecting a table, click the <table> tag down in the status bar.

- To split a single cell into two cells, right-click inside it, and in the context menu choose Table > Split Cell.

import tabular data p. 52

- Before importing, use your spreadsheet or word-processing program to save the data in comma- or tab-delimited form.

- Instead of using the Import Tabular Data button in the Data tab, you also can choose Insert > Table Objects > Import Tabular Data.

sort tables p. 55

- By default, the Options in the Sort Table dialog box are not checked, since you seldom want the header or footer included in the sort.

5. create links

The Web's magic comes largely from the hyperlink, which lets Web users jump from page to image to email to almost anywhere on the Internet. Links fall into two categories: internal links, which connect different items within your own Web site, and external links, which connect to items out on the larger Web. Before we begin linking some of the pages created in previous chapters, switch the Insert toolbar to the Common tab, which includes link-related buttons.

Add link   Add anchor link

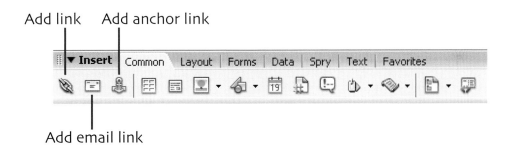

Add email link

link text internally

Dreamweaver makes creating links between pages on your Web site a point-and-click affair. (See extra bits on page 75.)

1 Open your home page and select text you want to link to another page on your Web site. (In our example, we are linking the word Europe in the Roman Holiday package to a day-by-day itinerary, tabular.html.)

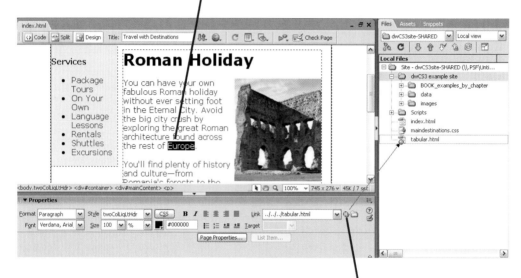

2 Make sure the Files panel and the Property Inspector are both visible.

3 Click the compass-like Point to File icon and drag the line that appears to your target file in the Files panel. Release your cursor and the file path to that file appears in the Link text window.

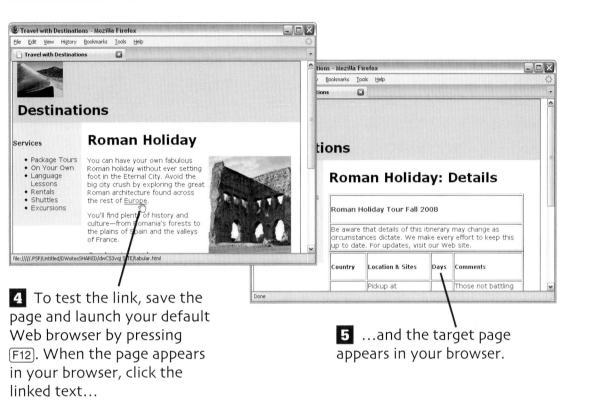

4 To test the link, save the page and launch your default Web browser by pressing F12. When the page appears in your browser, click the linked text...

5 ...and the target page appears in your browser.

link text externally

Links to items that are not part of your own Web site are called external links. While we use text in this example, you can create external links using images as well. (See extra bits on page 75.)

1 Make sure the Property Inspector is visible, then select the text you want to link to a page out on the Web.

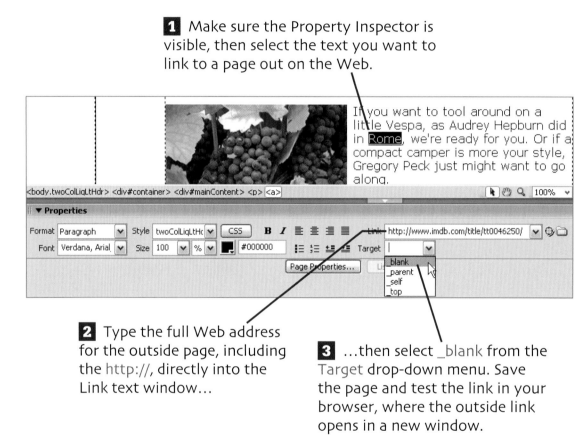

2 Type the full Web address for the outside page, including the http://, directly into the Link text window...

3 ...then select _blank from the Target drop-down menu. Save the page and test the link in your browser, where the outside link opens in a new window.

add email link

By embedding addresses in your email links, you make it easy for readers to send email to you and others listed on your Web site. Unfortunately, you also make it easier for spammers with Web-crawler programs to pick up that address and flood it with spam. For another approach, see create form on page 102.

1 Select the text on your page that you want to link to email. (In our example, we've selected Rentals from the page's sidebar of available services.)

2 Click the Email Link button under the Common tab of the Insert toolbar.

3 The selected text appears in the top field in the Email Link dialog box. Type the email address into the bottom field and click OK.

4 The text selected on your page becomes a link. Test it by saving the page, opening it in your Web browser, and clicking the link. Your default email program automatically creates a new message addressed to the email address on the Web page.

add anchor link

Anchor links enable Web visitors to jump to a specific spot within a long Web page, sparing readers from scrolling through it. You must first create an anchor to mark the particular spot in the target document. Then you create a link to that spot. (See extra bits on page 75.)

1 Open a Web page and click on the particular spot—not selecting the text itself—where you want to add an anchor link. (In our example, we're marking the start of the France section of tabular.html.)

2 Click the Named Anchor button in the Insert toolbar.

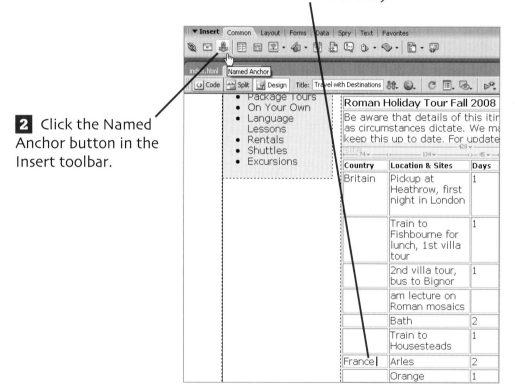

3 Type a distinctive name in the Named Anchor dialog box and click OK.

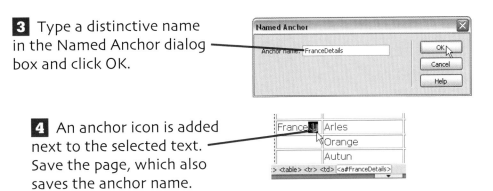

4 An anchor icon is added next to the selected text. Save the page, which also saves the anchor name.

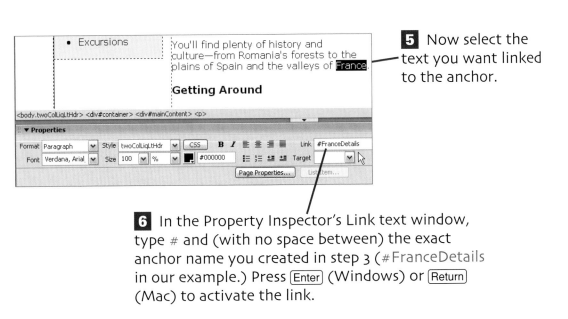

5 Now select the text you want linked to the anchor.

6 In the Property Inspector's Link text window, type # and (with no space between) the exact anchor name you created in step 3 (#FranceDetails in our example.) Press [Enter] (Windows) or [Return] (Mac) to activate the link.

create links

link image

Images are easy to spot on a page and easy to click, so don't limit yourself to creating just text links. Creating internal and external links with images works exactly as it does for text links.

1 With the Files panel and Property Inspector both visible, open the page containing the image you want to link to something, and select it.

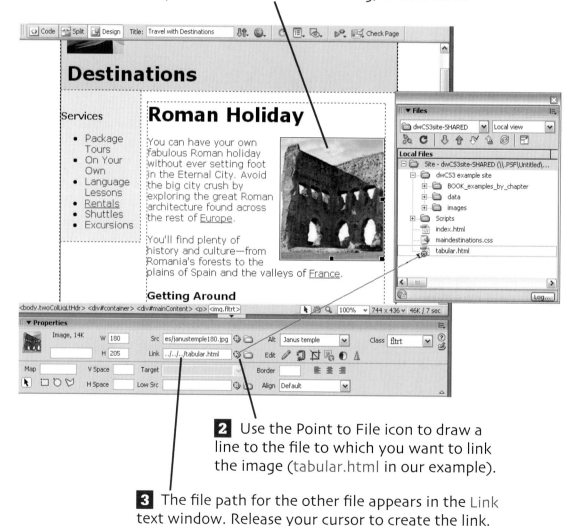

2 Use the Point to File icon to draw a line to the file to which you want to link the image (tabular.html in our example).

3 The file path for the other file appears in the Link text window. Release your cursor to create the link.

create image map

Image maps take the basic idea behind an image link and give it extra power by making it possible to link separate hot spots within the image to multiple files. It saves space on the page and provides an elegant, easy-to-understand interface for your site. (See extra bits on page 75 for a note about an image map bug.)

1 With the Property Inspector visible, select the image for which you want to create an image map. Type a name for the image map in the Map text window (Europe in our example).

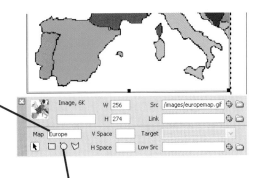

2 Based on the shape of the hot spot you'll be creating, click one of the three shape buttons (the Oval tool in our example).

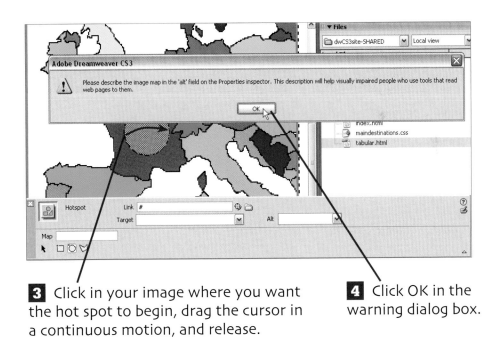

3 Click in your image where you want the hot spot to begin, drag the cursor in a continuous motion, and release.

4 Click OK in the warning dialog box.

create image map (cont.)

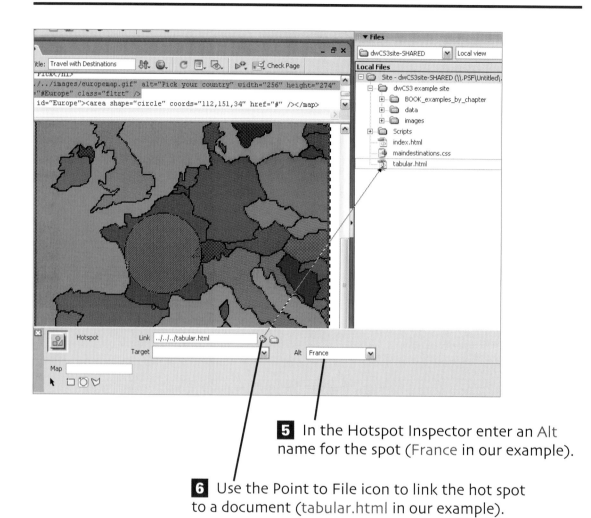

5 In the Hotspot Inspector enter an Alt name for the spot (France in our example).

6 Use the Point to File icon to link the hot spot to a document (tabular.html in our example).

7 If you need to adjust the hot spot's boundary, click any square-shaped handle and drag it to a new spot.

8 Repeat these steps for each hot spot you need to create. Be sure to add an Alt name for each hot spot to help you keep them straight.

create links

9 To test the link, save the page, and launch your default Web browser by pressing [F12]. Roll the cursor over any of the image's hot spots and the name of the linked file appears in the Status bar.

10 Click the spot and the linked page appears in your browser.

color site links

By default, unvisited Web links are blue and underlined while visited links are purple and underlined. Dreamweaver, however, makes it easy to change the color and style of all your links to match your Web site's overall look. Here we'll set colors for all four link states: unvisited link, visited, hover, and active. (See extra bits on page 75.)

1 Open your home page, make sure your CSS Styles tab is visible, and click the New CSS Rule button.

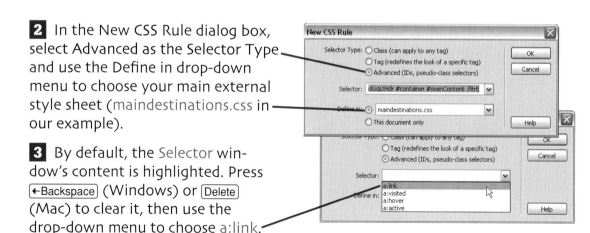

2 In the New CSS Rule dialog box, select Advanced as the Selector Type and use the Define in drop-down menu to choose your main external style sheet (maindestinations.css in our example).

3 By default, the Selector window's content is highlighted. Press `←Backspace` (Windows) or `Delete` (Mac) to clear it, then use the drop-down menu to choose a:link. Click OK to close the dialog box.

4 In the Type category, which is automatically selected, click the Color box and use the drop-down menu to choose a color for your hyperlinks.

5 Click OK to close the dialog box.

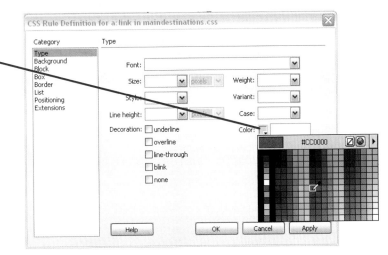

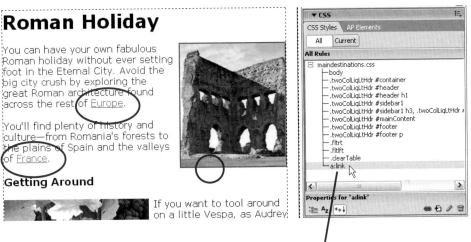

6 The new a:link rule is added to the style sheet list and the page's links assume the new color. But there are two problems: the links are underlined, when we don't want them to be, and the linked image shows a colored border, which we also don't want. We'll fix the underline problem first by double-clicking the a:link rule to reopen the rule definition dialog box.

color site links (cont.)

7 By default, the Type category remains selected. Change the Decoration checkbox from underline to none.

Roman Holiday

You can have your own fabulous Roman holiday without ever setting foot in the Eternal City. Avoid the big city crush by exploring the great Roman architecture found across the rest of Europe.

You'll find plenty of history and culture—from Romania's forests to the plains of Spain and the valleys of France.

Getting Around

If yo
on a

<Content> <p>

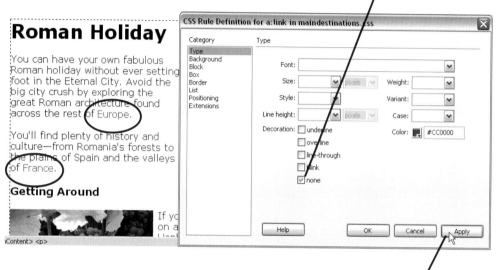

8 Position the dialog box so that you can see your page, click Apply, and the page links lose the underlines. Click OK to close the dialog box.

9 When the CSS Styles tab reappears, click the New CSS Rule button as you did in step 1.

10 In the New CSS Rule dialog box, set the Selector Type to Tag and use the Tag alphabetic pop-up menu to select img (for image). By default, Define in should still be set to your main external style sheet (maindestinations.css in our example).

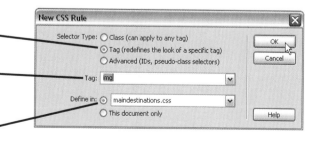

create links

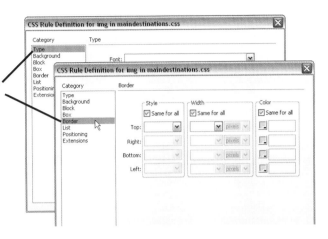

11 Change the category from Type to Border.

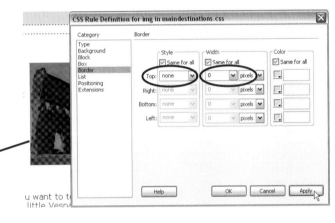

12 In the Style column, set the Top text window to none. In the Width column, type o (zero) in the Top window; the pixels measure then appears automatically. Position the dialog box so that you can see your page, click Apply, and the image's border disappears.

Roman Holiday

You can have your own fabulous Roman holiday without ever setting foot in the Eternal City. Avoid the big city crush by exploring the great Roman architecture found across the rest of Europe.

You'll find plenty of history and culture—from Romania's forests to the plains of Spain and the valleys of France.

Getting Around

If you want to tool around on a little Vespa, as Audrey

13 Click OK to close the dialog box, and the new img rule appears at the bottom of the CSS Styles tab. Choose File > Save All to save the changes to the content and style sheet.

create links   **73**

color site links (cont.)

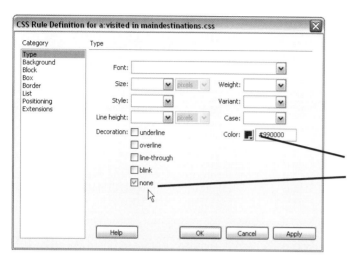

14 With those cleanups out of the way, repeat steps 1–6 to create and define rules for the remaining three link states: a:visited, a:hover, and a:active. Just remember while setting each state's link Color to also set Decoration to none at the same time.

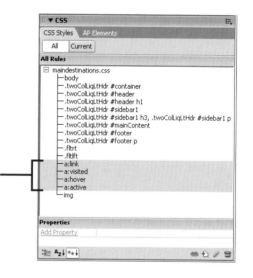

15 Choose File > Save All to save all your content and style changes. When you're done, all four link styles are listed in your main external style sheet (maindestinations.css in our example). These are applied to any hyperlinks in pages attached to the style sheet, as explained in the next chapter.

create links

extra bits

link text internally p. 60

- If the file to which you're linking is not already part of your Web site, click the Folder icon next to the Link drop-down menu and navigate to it. When Dreamweaver asks to import the file into the site, click Yes.

link text externally p. 62

- Selecting _blank from the Target drop-down menu opens a new window in the visitor's browser—ensuring that your site remains visible as the visitor looks at the external Web page.

add anchor link p. 64

- The anchor doesn't need to be tied to a text selection.

- Dreamweaver inserts an icon next to your anchor-link text just to help you spot it. It will not be visible on your Web site. To turn these icons off or on, choose View > Visual Aids > Invisible Elements.

create image map p. 67

- At press time, the polygon tool for creating image maps can't be used because of a software bug in version 9.0, build 3481. Choose Help > Updates to see if a newer version is available.

- Image map names should not include any blank spaces or special characters.

- The hot spot need not exactly match the underlying shape. Just cover the portion your visitors will most likely click.

- If you can't arrange your document windows to point directly to an anchor, click the folder button to reach the file. At the end of the file name selected in the Link text window, type a # and the exact name of the anchor (without a space).

- A hot spot can link to an internal or external file.

color site links p. 70

- You also could create the links as their own separate style sheet. The drawback is you have to attach it to all your pages. By creating the link styles within the main style sheet, that's one less style sheet to attach.

6. use style sheets

In previous chapters, you saw how Cascading Style Sheets (CSS) save you time in creating and formatting pages. Using those examples, you learned how to change and create style rules. In this chapter, we go a bit deeper, formatting elements based on their use or context.

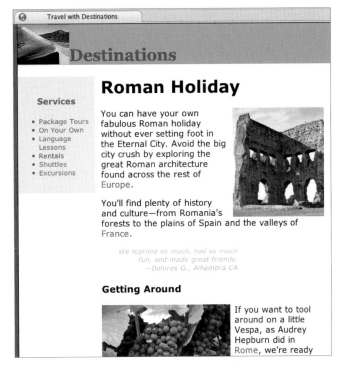

You'll learn to create a variety of styles to cover virtually all your needs. Tag-based styles, also known as element-based styles, apply to a specific HTML element, such as every h1 or li tag. Context-based styles enable you to apply a style when a certain tag appears in a specific context, such as the page's header or sidebar. Finally, class-based styles are not pegged to a particular tag and, so, can be applied to multiple items anywhere in a page. If you want to learn still more about CSS after reading this chapter, check out Peachpit's Dreamweaver CS3: Visual QuickStart Guide on page xiv.

using the css styles tab

Dreamweaver conveniently puts everything you need for creating and managing style sheets in the CSS Styles tab. Along with the Files tab, it's something you'll always want visible. In contrast, you're unlikely to ever use the AP Elements tab, which is grouped in the same CSS panel. (See extra bits on page 91.)

In All rules mode

In Current rules mode

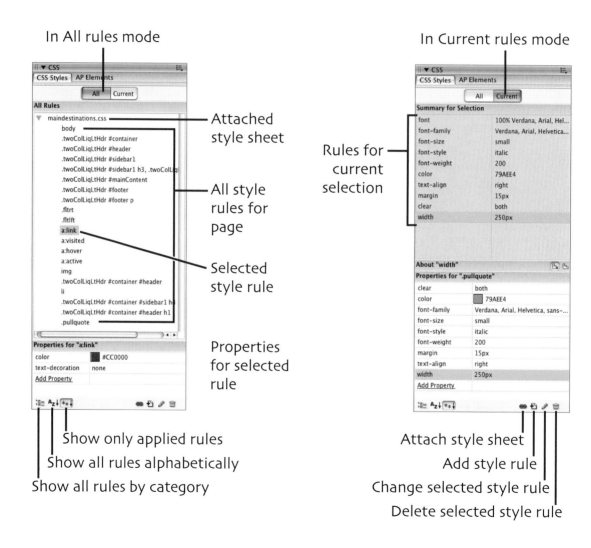

Attached style sheet

All style rules for page

Selected style rule

Rules for current selection

Properties for selected rule

Show only applied rules
Show all rules alphabetically
Show all rules by category

Attach style sheet
Add style rule
Change selected style rule
Delete selected style rule

use style sheets

To open the CSS Styles tab, choose Windows > CSS Styles or click the CSS button in the Property Inspector.

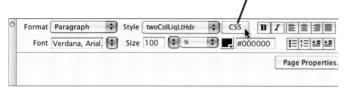

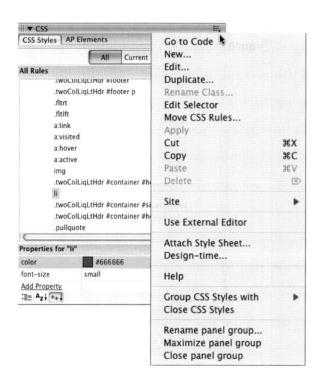

Use the drop-down menu at the top right of the CSS panel group for such common tasks as duplicating a style rule or expanding and closing the group.

use style sheets

detach, attach style sheets

From the beginning of this book, we've been using pages already attached to a style sheet (maindestinations.css in our examples). Let's detach a style sheet from a page to see how different unattached pages look, and then reattach it.

1 Make sure the CSS Styles tab is visible (Windows > CSS Styles) with the All button selected. Open your page (index_startChap06.html in our example).

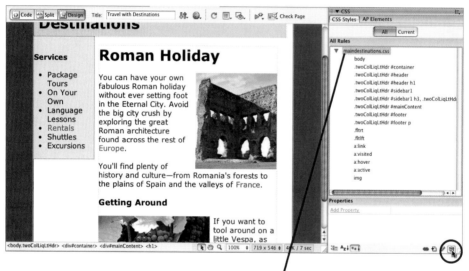

2 Select the style sheet in the CSS Styles tab (maindestinations.css in our example) and click the Delete button at the bottom (the Trash can).

use style sheets

3 The style sheet is no longer listed in the CSS Styles tab (don't worry, it still exists), and the page loses most of its formatting. This simple top-to-bottom stacking of elements is called the page's natural flow since there's no style sheet to float items to the left or right.

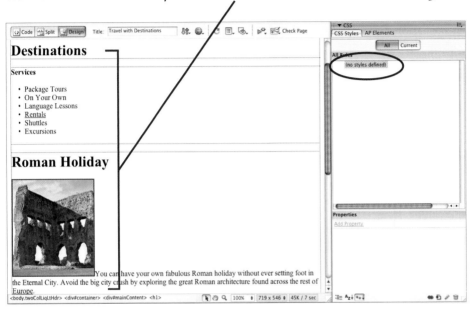

4 Let's reattach the previous style sheet. This process is the same one you'd use to change the look by attaching another style sheet instead. Start by clicking the chain-link Attach button in the CSS Styles tab.

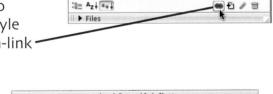

5 Click Browse to navigate to where the desired style sheet resides. (In our example, it's maindestinations.css at the site's top level.) Leave Link selected and click OK. The page changes to reflect the style sheet's formatting, which in this example is exactly what we started with in step 1.

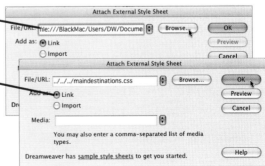

use style sheets

create tag-based style

Tag-based styles affect every instance of a selected HTML element. Create a list style, for example, and it's applied to every list tag in every page attached to that style sheet.

1 Open your page (index_startChapo6.html in our example). Select the text in any list (not the list's headline however). Right-click ([Option]-click for single-button Macs) and choose CSS Styles > New in the context menu. (Or click the Add CSS Rule button, the plus, at the bottom of the CSS Styles tab.)

2 In the New CSS Rule dialog box, select Tag as the Selector Type.

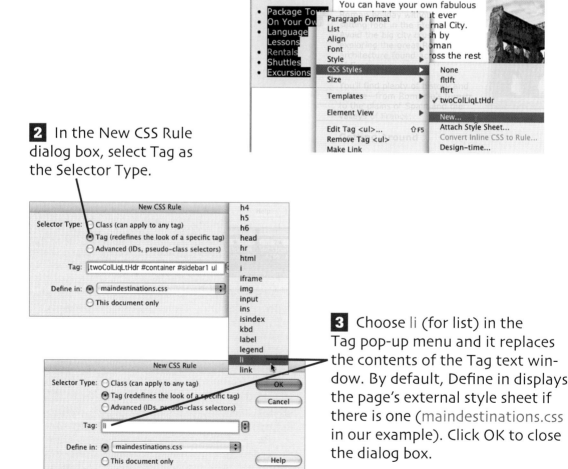

3 Choose li (for list) in the Tag pop-up menu and it replaces the contents of the Tag text window. By default, Define in displays the page's external style sheet if there is one (maindestinations.css in our example). Click OK to close the dialog box.

use style sheets

4 In the Type category, set the Size and Color. (In our example, small and #666666, a gray, are chosen to keep the list from competing visually with the page's main content.)

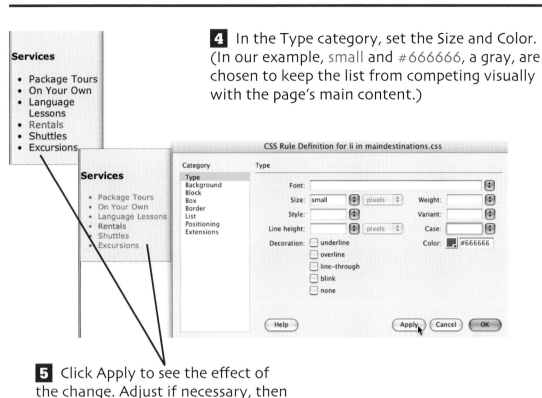

5 Click Apply to see the effect of the change. Adjust if necessary, then click OK to close the dialog box.

6 Choose File > Save All and the new style for lists is applied to every list linked to that external style sheet.

create context-based style

You're not limited to applying tag-based styles to every instance of an HTML element. You also can define such styles so that they're applied only when that particular element appears in a specific part, or division, of a page. These context-based styles are particularly powerful when used with Dreamweaver's predesigned layouts, which use div tags to mark the page's different divisions. (See extra bits on page 91.)

1 Make sure the CSS Styles tab is visible, and open your page (index_startChap06. html in our example). Select the heading for the list used in the previous steps (Services in our example's sidebar list).

2 Right-click ([Option]-click for single-button Macs) and choose CSS Styles > New in the context menu. (Or click the Add CSS Rule plus button at the bottom of the CSS Styles tab.)

3 Let's look at what's inside the Selector text window. In our example, it reads: .twoColLiqLtHdr #container #sidebar1 h4. The first bit of code, .twoColLiqLtHdr, refers to the layout you first chose on page 12, which uses a two-

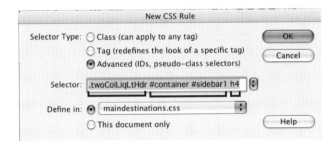

column liquid layout with a header. The # leading off the next two bits of code tells you these are page divisions marked with specific ID tags: container and sidebar1. Every CSS layout includes a #container. The #sidebar1 marks the sidebar holding the Services heading, which as the code tells us is styled as an h4 (Heading 4).

Here's the cool part about all this: Dreamweaver has automatically identified Heading 4's context. That's why Advanced is already selected. All you have to do is click OK.

use style sheets

4 In the CSS Rule Definition dialog box that appears, use the left-side categories to precisely define how the selected element should look in this particular context. (In our example, we use the Type category to set the color to #666666 to match the list color, and the Block category to set the heading alignment to center.)

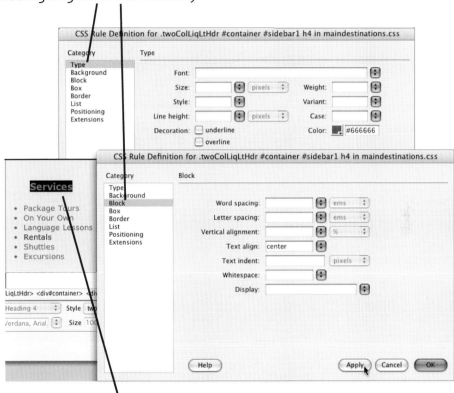

5 Click Apply to see the effect of the change. Adjust if necessary, then click OK to close the dialog box.

context-based style (cont.)

6 The new context-based rule is added to the style sheet in the CSS Styles tab. Look at the tab's existing styles and you can see the same rules at play. For example, the .twoColLiqLtHdr #footer p rule is a context-based style for paragraphs in the footer division.

7 Let's use context-based styles to quickly make some other needed changes to our example. Click in the header's Heading 1 (Destinations). Right-click and choose CSS Styles > New in the context menu.

8 In the New CSS Rule dialog box, Dreamweaver automatically selects Advanced and generates a context-based Selector for the Heading 1, so click OK.

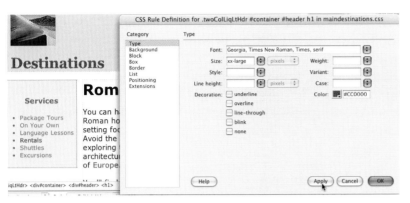

9 In the Type category, set the Font to the Georgia, Times New Roman, Times, serif family, the Size to xx-large, and the Color to #CC0000. Click Apply to see the effect of the change, and click OK to close the dialog box.

10 Let's make two more changes involving the header. Select the header's logo image (dunelogo100.jpg in our example). In the Property Inspector set its alignment to Left.

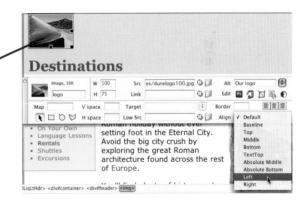

11 Click anywhere in the header, then click <div#header> in the status bar to select all of the header.

12 Switch the CSS Styles tab from All to Current and double-click the .twoColLiqLtHdr #header rule.

use style sheets

context-based style (cont.)

13 In the Background category, click the Background color drop-down menu and use the eye dropper that appears to select a color in the logo image that you'd like use for the header's background.

14 Now select the Box category and change all the Padding values to 0. Click OK to close the rule definition dialog box.

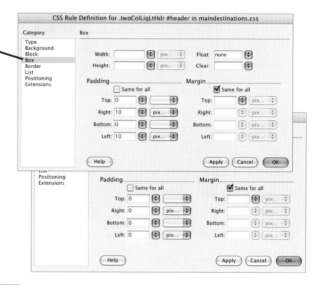

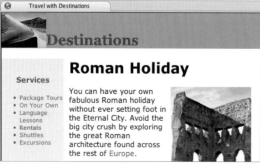

15 Choose File > Save All to save your changes to the page and the attached style sheet. Press F12 to preview the changes in your default Web browser.

use style sheets

create class-based style

Class-based styles can be applied to multiple items on a page. In our example, we create a style for formatting quotes by customers. But class-based styles also are handy for such things as applying the same color to various elements to give your site a unified look.

1 Open any page to which you've already attached your main css style sheet. (In our example, we're using index_startChap06.html, which is attached to maindestinations.css.) In the CSS Styles tab, click the Add CSS Rule button at the bottom of the tab.

2 In the New CSS Rule dialog box, select Class as the Selector Type. In the Name text window, type pullquote and click OK to close the dialog box.

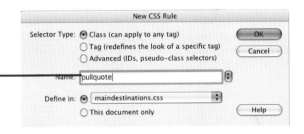

3 Use the various categories in the rule definition dialog box to define the look of your pull quote. (In our example, we use the Type category to set the Font to Verdana, Arial, Helvetica, sans-serif, the Size to small, the Weight to 200, the Style to italic, and the Color to 79AEE4 to match the header's new color.)

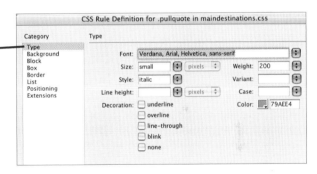

4 In our example, we use the Block category to make just one change: setting Text align to right.

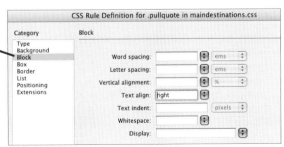

class-based style (cont.)

5 In our example, we use the Box category to set the Width to 250 (pixels), the Clear to both, and the Margin to 15 (pixels) all the way around.

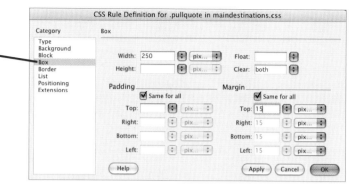

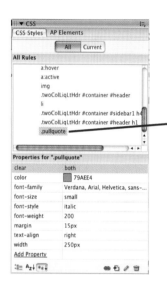

6 Click Apply to see the effect of your changes. Adjust if necessary, then click OK to close the dialog box. The new rule appears in the CSS Styles tab with the properties you assigned.

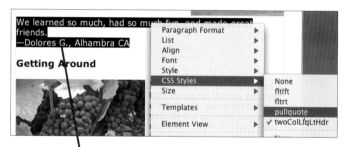

7 To apply the new class-based rule, select the text you want formatted as a pull quote. (In our example, there are two text areas: the first just above the Getting Around heading, the other at the bottom of the main content area.) Right-click (Option-click for single-button Macs) the text, and choose CSS Styles > pullquote in the context menu.

8 Click anywhere in the page to see the effect. Choose File > Save All to save the page and the style sheet.

extra bits

using the css styles tab p. 78

- By default, the AP Elements tab is grouped with the CSS Styles tab within the CSS panel group. It controls absolutely positioned layout elements, which are not covered in this book.

create context-based style p. 84

- When creating a context-based heading, don't undermine the relative sizing inherent in headings where heading 1 is the largest and heading 6 the smallest. For example, it makes sense to set a heading 1 to xx-large since it's the largest size available. But it'd be potentially confusing to set a heading 1 to xx-small since there'd be nothing smaller available for headings 2–6.

- Another common use of a context-based style might involve selecting text inside a table and creating a smaller, sans-serif style that would apply only to text in tables.

- To get a deeper understanding of context-based styles, select any rule with a # (ID tag) in the CSS Styles tab and take a look at the properties listed in the bottom half of the tab. From there, it's a small step to creating all sorts of context-based styles for your pages.

7. add interactivity

One of the great advantages of Web pages over printed pages is their ability to respond to viewers' actions. When used with restraint, this interactivity can entice your visitors to explore your site more thoroughly. Whether it's building a menu that responds to cursor movements or simply creating a form for collecting information from visitors, Dreamweaver's tools make it easy.

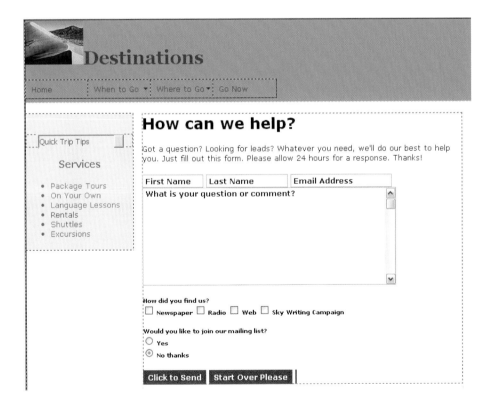

add navigation menu

Dreamweaver CS3 includes a new set of tools called Spry widgets. Combining JavaScript and CSS, most of these widgets lie well beyond the scope of this beginner book. But one, the Spry Menu Bar, helps you create fly-out menus even if you're not a big-league code jockey. (See extra bits on page 108.)

1 Open your home page (index_startChap07.html in our example) and switch the Insert toolbar to the Spry tab.

2 In the header, click after the heading (Destinations in our example) and press Enter (Windows) or Return (Mac) to give yourself some space for the menu.

3 In the Spry tab, click the Spry Menu Bar button. Select the Horizontal button and click OK.

4 When the menu bar appears, select and replace each label within the menu itself or use the text windows in the Property Inspector. (In our example, the first items are replaced by Home and When to Go.)

add interactivity

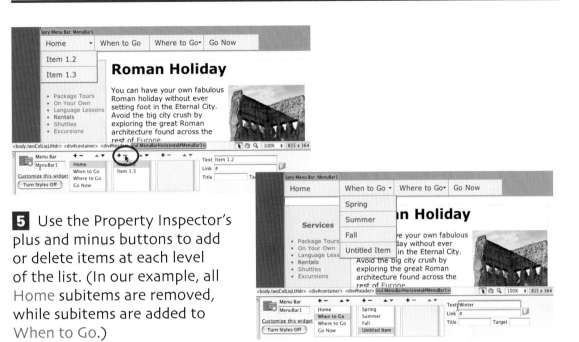

5 Use the Property Inspector's plus and minus buttons to add or delete items at each level of the list. (In our example, all Home subitems are removed, while subitems are added to When to Go.)

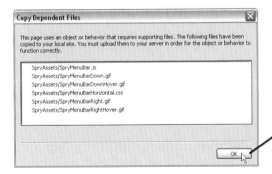

6 Choose File > Save All and click OK when Dreamweaver asks to copy a series of script and image files to your site.

add interactivity

add navigation menu (cont.)

7 Press [F12] to preview the menu in your default Web browser.

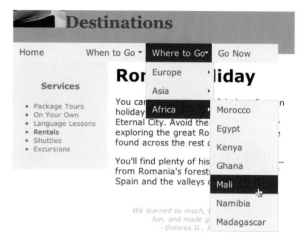

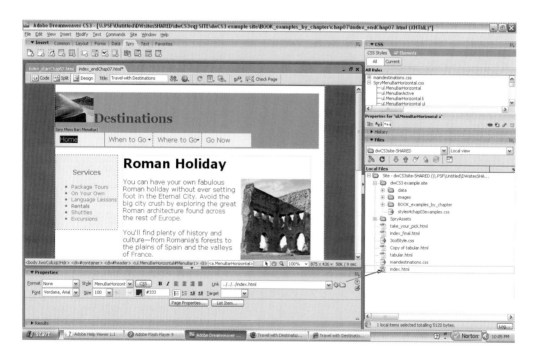

8 Return to Dreamweaver where, if necessary, you can edit the menu labels right away (or later if you prefer). To link a label to its target page, select it in the menu and use the Property Inspector's Point to File button as explained on page 60.

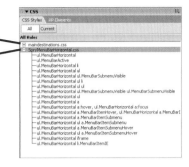

9 To change the menu bar's formatting, collapse your main CSS in the CSS Styles tab and expand the newly added SpryMenuBarHorizontal.css. While its many rules may seem daunting, only a handful control the menu bar's text size and coloring.

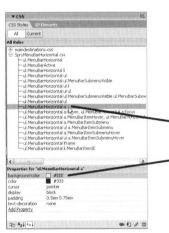

10 Start by selecting ul.MenuBarHorizontal a in the CSS Styles tab, which controls the menu's background and text color.

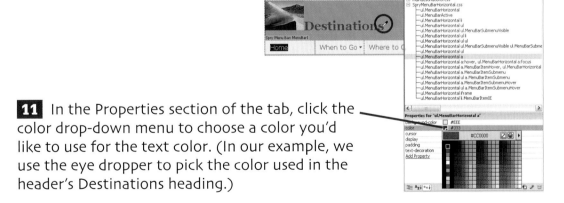

11 In the Properties section of the tab, click the color drop-down menu to choose a color you'd like to use for the text color. (In our example, we use the eye dropper to pick the color used in the header's Destinations heading.)

add navigation menu (cont.)

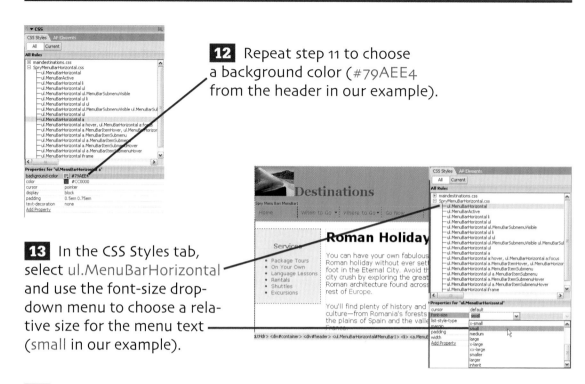

12 Repeat step 11 to choose a background color (#79AEE4 from the header in our example).

13 In the CSS Styles tab, select ul.MenuBarHorizontal and use the font-size drop-down menu to choose a relative size for the menu text (small in our example).

14 In the CSS Styles tab, select the rule that begins with ul.MenuBarHorizontal a.MenuBarItemHover and click the color drop-down menu to choose a color for when a visitor's cursor hovers over the menu text (#FFFFFF in our example).

15 Choose File > Save All, then press F12 to preview the changes in your default Web browser.

---

add interactivity

add jump menu

A jump menu is one of the most useful of the many behaviors you can add to a page because it gives your users lots of navigation information in a small space. By clicking the menu, users can choose among a variety of links to which they can jump directly. (See extra bits on page 108.)

1 Before you begin, create the pages to which you want to link; Dreamweaver doesn't offer a way to create them on the fly while building the jump menu. Open your home page (index_startChap07.html in our example) and switch the Insert toolbar to the Forms tab.

2 In the sidebar, click before the heading (Services in our example). In the Forms tab, click the Jump Menu button.

3 Item1 is automatically added to the menu. Use the Text window to rename this first item, typically with something that clues visitors to the jump menu's contents since this line appears by default. Leave it unlinked.

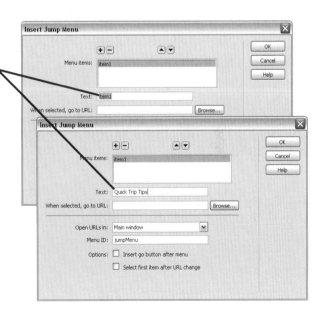

add jump menu (cont.)

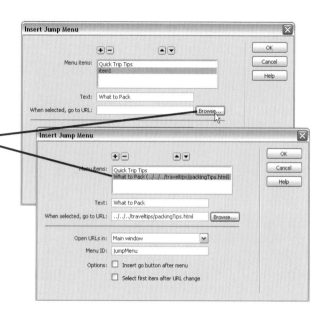

4 Click the ⊞ button to add another item to the menu list, use the Text window to rename it, and click Browse to link the item to a page.

5 Continue adding, naming, and linking items until you finish your menu list. If you need to reorder an item, select it and use the up or down arrow buttons to move it. If your first item is a label rather than a link (Quick Trip Tips in our example), choose the Select first item after URL change box to put that item at the top of the jump menu. Click OK and the jump menu appears on the page.

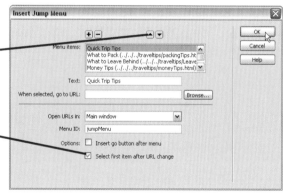

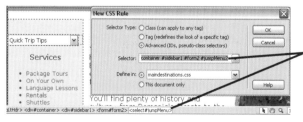

6 To change the menu's appearance, click <select#jumpMenu> in the bottom status bar. In the CSS Styles tab, click the Add CSS Rule button to create a new context-based style for the jump menu. Click OK to begin defining the rule.

add interactivity

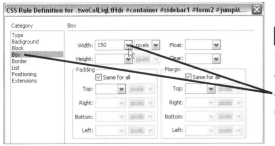

7 Based on what you learned in Chapter 6 about CSS, you can build as detailed a rule as you like. Be sure, at least, to use the Box category to define the jump menu's width so that it fits within the sidebar.

8 When you finish defining the rule, click OK to close the definition dialog box and your restyled menu appears with its new formatting.

9 Choose File > Save All, then press F12 to preview the changes in your default Web browser.

create form

Forms enable you to collect information from your visitors using simple text areas and buttons. As mentioned on page 63, they also offer you a way to receive messages from visitors without posting an email address on the Web site that gets grabbed by Web-crawling spammers. Before starting, check with the administrator for your Internet Service Provider or Web site to find out what System CGI to use in step 5. (See extra bits on page 108.)

1 Create a new page for your site by duplicating the one you've been using and renaming it form.html (form_startChap07.html in our example). Replace the main content area with heading and text explaining the form.

2 Switch the Insert toolbar to the Forms tab. Click the Form button. A blank form with a red dashed border appears on the page.

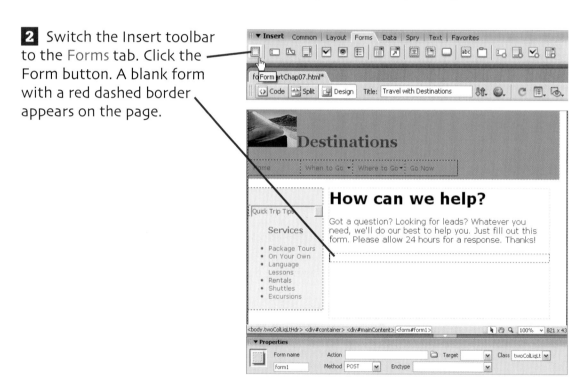

3 Select and cut your header and introductory text, then paste it inside the red border, which sits within the yellow dashed border. Press Enter (Windows) or Return (Mac) to start a new line.

How can we help?

Got a question? Looking for leads? Whatever you need, we'll do our best to help you. Just fill out this form. Please allow 24 hours for a response. Thanks!

4 In the Property Inspector, replace the generic name assigned to the form with something that indicates its purpose.

5 Type into the Action window the System CGI recommended for your Web server.

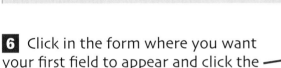

6 Click in the form where you want your first field to appear and click the Text Field button in the Forms tab.

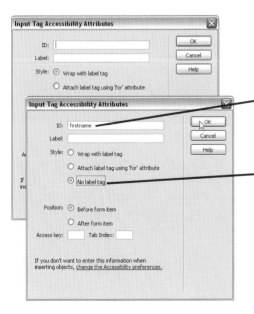

7 The Input Tag Accessibility Attributes dialog box appears each time you use the Text Field button. Type in an ID that helps you recognize this field's purpose (firstname in our example since that's what it will hold). Don't use blank spaces or special characters since the ID is used in scripts, which don't recognize such characters. Select No label tag for a cleaner look, as explained in the next step. Click OK to close the dialog box.

add interactivity

create form (cont.)

8 The new field is blank when it first appears in the form. In the Property Inspector, use the Char width and Init val text windows to adjust the field's width and create an initial value that appears as a defacto label inside the field.

9 Repeat steps 6–8 for each text field you want added to the form.

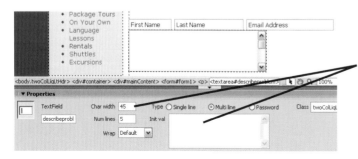

10 To create a large text field for comments, click the Textarea button in the Forms tab. Create an ID when the Input Tag Accessibility Attributes dialog box appears, and click OK to close the dialog box.

11 When the larger field appears in your form, use the Property Inspector to set its width and initial value.

add interactivity

12 To create a multiple-choice question for readers, type the question below the previous text area. Press ⟨⇧Shift⟩⟨Enter⟩ (Windows) or ⟨⇧Shift⟩⟨Return⟩ (Mac) to start a new line and click the Checkbox button in the Forms tab.

13 Create an ID in the Input Tag Accessibility Attributes dialog box. In this case, create a label and select the After form item position. Since this form uses a checkbox, there's no room to tuck the label inside it. Click OK.

14 When the checkbox and label appear, check the Property Inspector to make sure that its Initial state is set to Unchecked.

15 Repeat steps 12–14 until you create all the choices for the question.

create form (cont.)

16 To create a single-choice question for readers, type the question in the form. Press ⇧Shift Enter (Windows) or ⇧Shift Return (Mac) to start a new line and click the Radio Group button in the Forms tab.

17 Give the Radio Group a distinctive Name and rename each button using the Label column. If you need more items, click the ⊕ button. Click OK when you're done.

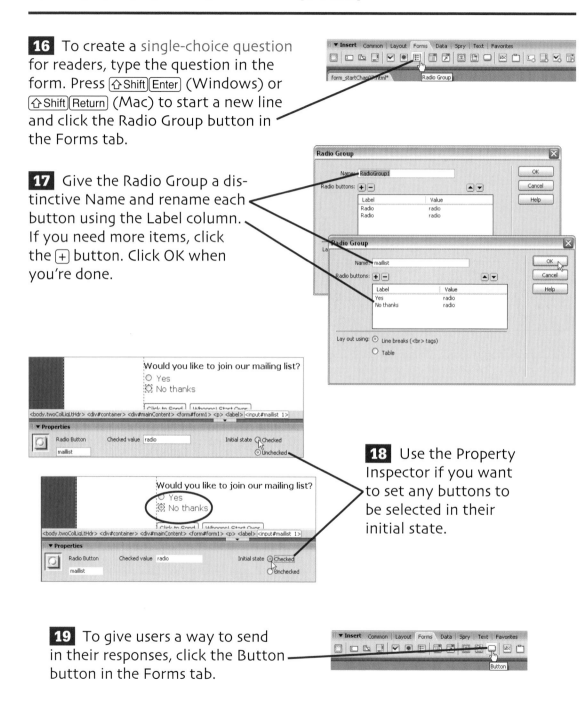

18 Use the Property Inspector if you want to set any buttons to be selected in their initial state.

19 To give users a way to send in their responses, click the Button button in the Forms tab.

20 Create an ID when the Input Tag Accessibility Attributes dialog box appears, and click OK to close the dialog box.

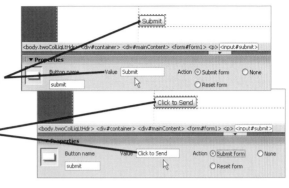

21 The new button is named Submit when it first appears in the form. Use the Value window to create a more helpful label (Click to Send in our example). By default, the Action is set to Submit form.

22 Repeat steps 19–21 to give users a second button to start over with the form. Again, use the Property Inspector's Value window to relabel the button (Start Over Please in our example). Be sure to change the Action to Reset form.

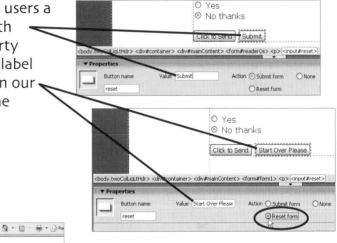

23 Choose File > Save All, then press F12 to preview the form in your default Web browser. Use the CSS Styles tab to format the form to reflect your Web site's overall look and design, as we did on page 93.

add interactivity

extra bits

add navigation menu p. 94

- In step 3, if you choose Vertical instead of Horizontal, all the rules in steps 9–14 are listed as MenuBarVertical... instead of MenuBarHorizontal.... Otherwise, the rest of the steps are the same.

- In step 14, the background color for the hover state was left the same, though you can change it if you want the rollover response to be more dramatic.

add jump menu p. 99

- In step 2, you also can choose Insert > Form > Jump Menu.

create form p. 102

- Use checkboxes when you want users to be able to pick more than one choice. Use radio buttons when you want users to pick just a single item.

add interactivity

8. reuse items to save time

Think of the Assets tab in the Files panel group as Dreamweaver's grand central timesaver. It automatically lists which images, color swatches, and external links you use on your site. If you want to use those items again, the Assets tab makes it easy to quickly find what you need. The Assets tab also includes library items, another major timesaver.

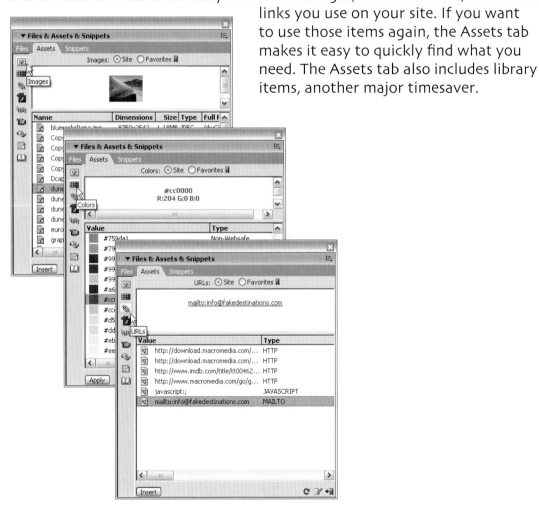

create a favorite

By creating favorites from the lists generated by the Assets tab, you always have your most-used items handy.

1 Press (F11) to open the Assets tab and make sure the Site radio button is selected.

2 Select a category button in the left-hand column. (In our example, we've chosen the Images button at the top of the column because with so many images used, creating a shorter favorites list is essential.)

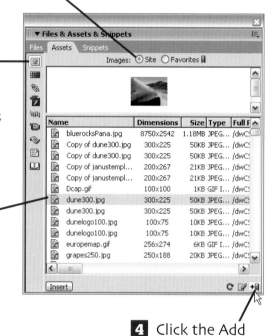

3 Select the image file you want to mark as a favorite.

4 Click the Add Favorite button at the bottom.

5 The first time you add a favorite, Dreamweaver displays a reminder dialog box telling you how to see favorites. To keep it from appearing each and every time you add a favorite, check Don't show me this message again and click OK. The image you marked is added to the list of favorite images.

reuse items to save time

use a favorite

With a favorites list, you save yourself from constantly digging through your Files tab.

1 Press F11 to open the Assets tab and click the Favorites radio button, and select a left-hand category button.

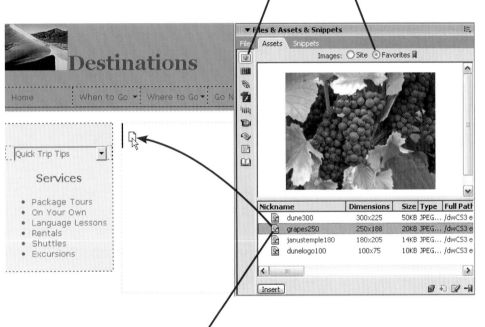

2 Select an image in the favorites list and drag it onto the page were you want it to appear.

create a library item

Make library items of anything you use repeatedly. It can be something simple like a 2 x 400-pixel rule. Or it can be as elaborate as the contents of a header. Short or long, the real benefit of a library item comes when you need to make a change—change it once and all pages using it automatically update. (See extra bits on page 116.)

1 Select the Library category button in the Assets tab of the Files panel.

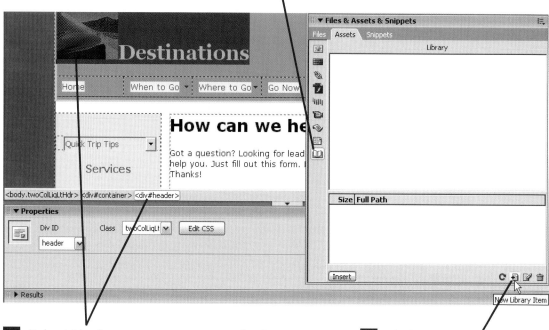

2 Select the item you want to make into a library item. (In our example, it's the contents of the header, which we selected by clicking <div#header> in the status bar.)

3 Click the New Library Item button at the bottom of the Assets tab.

reuse items to save time

4 Click OK when Dreamweaver warns that the library item cannot include the styling from the original page. However, leave Don't warn me again unchecked because you want to be reminded that this library item always needs to be reconnected to the original style sheet.

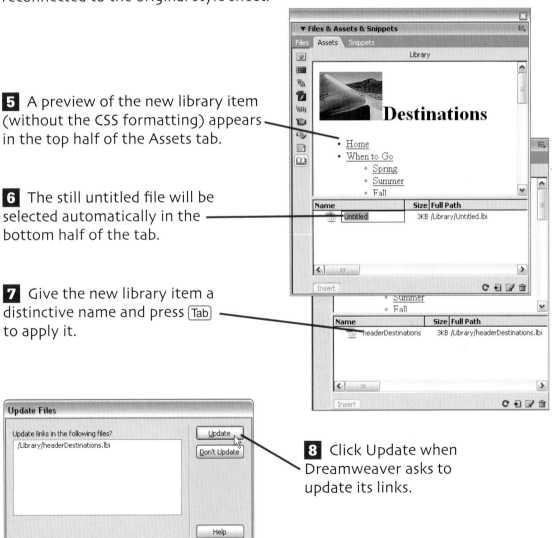

5 A preview of the new library item (without the CSS formatting) appears in the top half of the Assets tab.

6 The still untitled file will be selected automatically in the bottom half of the tab.

7 Give the new library item a distinctive name and press Tab to apply it.

8 Click Update when Dreamweaver asks to update its links.

edit library item

In this example, we want to change the copyright notice.

1 To fix it, click the Edit button at the bottom of the Assets tab.

2 When the library item appears, make your correction.

3 Save the changes and when Dreamweaver asks if it should change any pages containing this library item, click Update. When a second dialog box appears listing which pages were updated, click Close.

The Asset tab's preview of the library item updates to reflect the changes. Close the edited library page to get it out of your way.

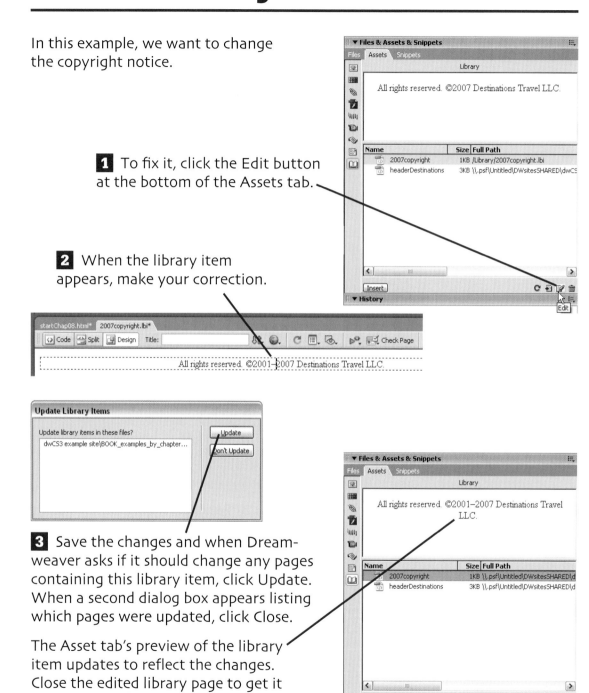

reuse items to save time

insert library item

Inserting a library item works similarly to adding a favorite to a page.

1 With the Assets tab of the Files panel open and visible, click in the open page where you want to place the selected library item or select an item you want replaced by the library item.

`<body.twoColLiqLtHdr> <div#container> <div#footer> <p>`

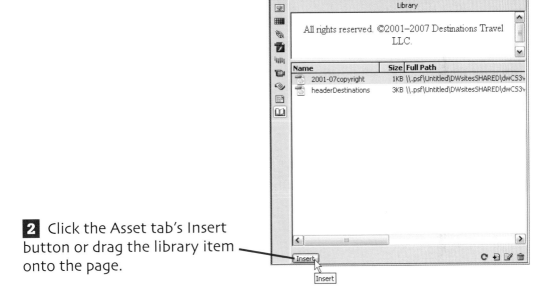

2 Click the Asset tab's Insert button or drag the library item onto the page.

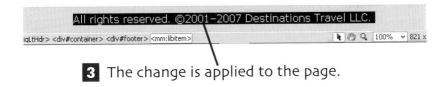

`iqLtHdr> <div#container> <div#footer> <mm:libitem>`

3 The change is applied to the page.

extra bits

create a library item p. 112

- While library items contain no styling themselves, they can contain references to style sheets. Use external style sheets to keep library items consistently styled, as explained in Chapter 6.

- Dreamweaver automatically adds the .lbi suffix to a library item file name, designating the file as a library item.

9. publish site

Finally, you're ready to put your pages on the Web, a process sometimes called publishing since they'll become available for anyone to read. Dreamweaver's expanded Files tab displays files on the remote Web server, along with those on your local machine. It plays a key role in helping you keep track of which files are where and when they were last changed.

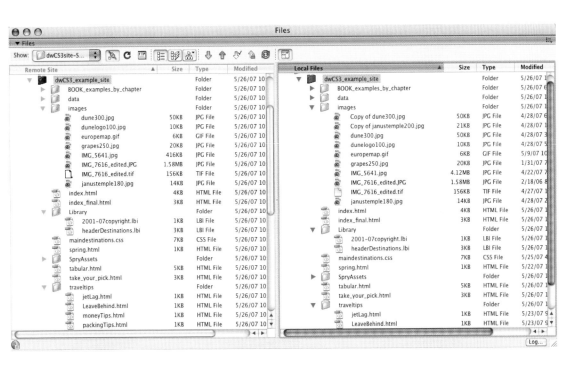

add search terms

It's easy for you to help Web search engines highlight your site if you enter a succinct description, along with multiple keywords, in the home page. Dreamweaver places this information in the page's hidden head code. (See extra bits on page 129.)

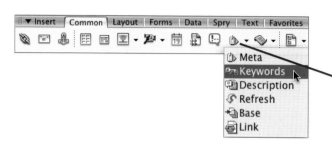

1 Open your home page and switch the Insert toolbar to the Common tab. Click the button that looks like a luggage tag and choose Keywords from its drop-down menu.

2 When the Keywords dialog box appears, type words that you think people might use to search for your site. Once you're done, click OK to close the dialog box.

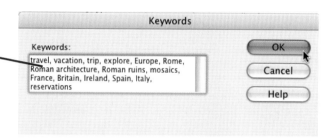

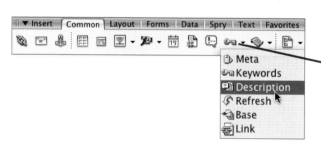

3 In the Common tab, click the same button which now looks like a key, reflecting your last choice, and choose Description from its drop-down menu.

4 When the Description dialog box appears, type in a short paragraph that sums up the purpose of your Web site and the products it displays. Once you're done, click OK to close the dialog box.

5 If you want to see the otherwise hidden keywords and description, click the Split button. The terms appear as part of the meta data in the page's head code.

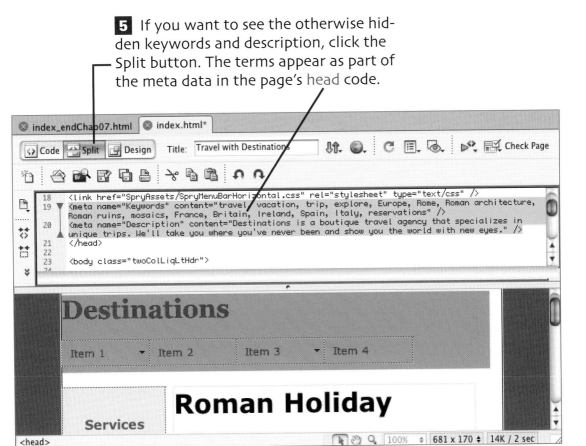

check and fix links

Few things are more frustrating for Web users than broken links. Dreamweaver can check your entire site in seconds and save everyone hours of frustration.

1 Choose Site > Check Links Site-wide. The Link Checker tab in the Results panel lists any pages with broken links.

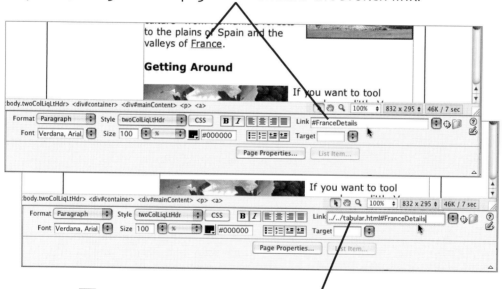

2 Double-click any file listed and Dreamweaver opens the Property Inspector, along with the page that contains the broken link.

3 Use the Property Inspector's Link text field to correct the mistake by typing in the correct link or redrawing the link with the Point to File button.

4 Once you make the fix, save the page and the Results panel automatically removes the broken link from its list. Repeat until you've fixed all broken links.

explore the files panel

The Files panel serves as your main tool to put files from your local site on to the Web server that will host your files, known as the remote site. You also use it to get any of your remote files if, for example, you've accidentally deleted their local site counterparts. (See extra bits on page 129.)

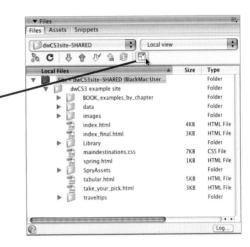

Normally the Files panel only shows your local files. Click the Expand/Collapse button to see them along with your remote Web site's files.

The toolbar running above the file listings contains all the buttons needed to move files between the two locations.

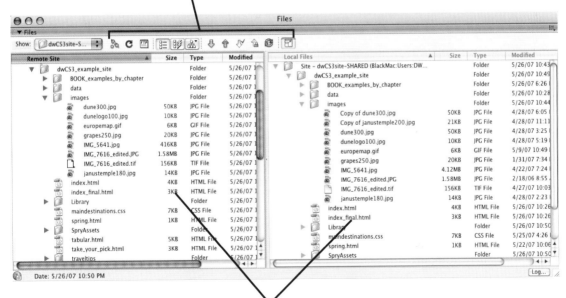

The expanded view of the Files panel shows your remote and local files.

explore the files panel (cont.)

Click the Connect/Disconnect button to open or close a live connection to the remote Web site.

Click the Get files button to move selected files from the remote site to the local site.

Click the Put files button to move selected files from your local site to the remote site.

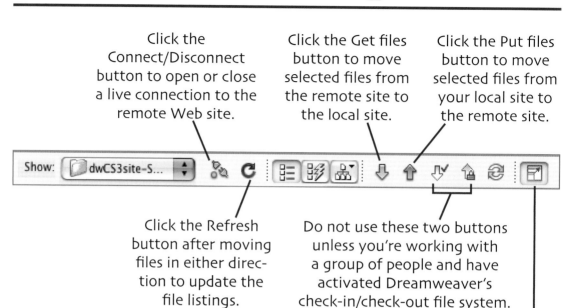

Show: dwCS3site-S...

Click the Refresh button after moving files in either direction to update the file listings.

Do not use these two buttons unless you're working with a group of people and have activated Dreamweaver's check-in/check-out file system.

The Expand/Collapse button lets you see the remote and local files, or just the local files.

set up remote site

After double-checking your files, you're ready to add the details about the remote site. Your computer is the local site, whose details you defined on page 7. (See extra bits on page 129.)

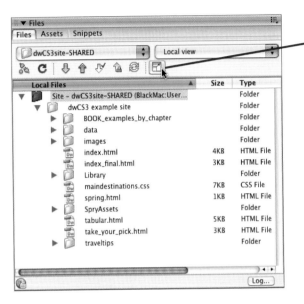

1 In the Files tab, click the Expand/Collapse button.

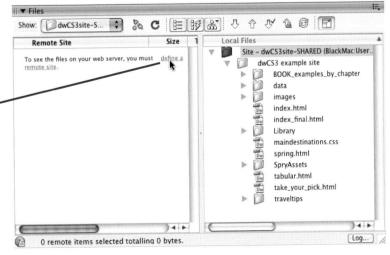

2 In the Remote Site panel, click the define a remote site link.

set up remote site (cont.)

3 The Advanced view appears in the Site Definition dialog box with the Remote Info category automatically selected. Choose FTP in the Access drop-down menu.

4 Fill in the FTP address for your new site, based on information provided by the firm hosting your site.

5 You don't have to specify which folder will contain the site, but it can help keep your site better organized. (In our example, we've created a special folder, dwCS3_VQJ_examples, for storing this book's example files.)

6 Fill in your login and password, again based on the information from your Web host.

7 Select Use passive FTP unless your Web host firm specifically tells you not to do so.

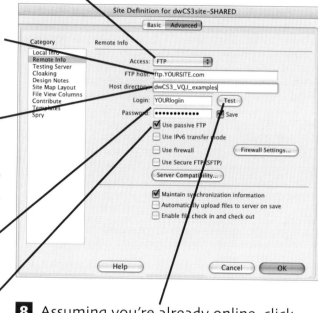

8 Assuming you're already online, click Test and it will take only a moment for Dreamweaver to determine if the connection is working.

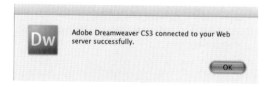

9 If the test connection works, click OK to close the message dialog box. Close the Site Definition dialog box by clicking OK.

publish site

connect to remote site

Having set up the remote site, you're ready to connect to it.

1 Unless you have an always-on connection to the Internet, activate your computer's dial-up connection now.

3 Once the view expands, click the Connect button.

2 Return to Dreamweaver, make sure the Files panel is visible, and click the Expand/Collapse button.

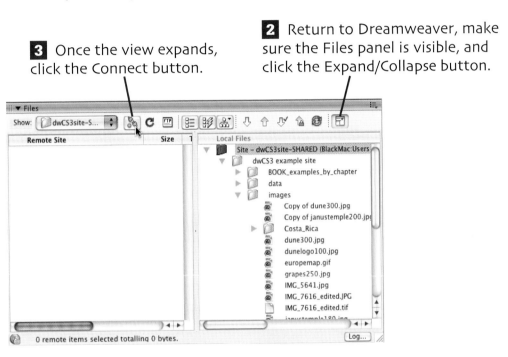

4 The status dialog box appears briefly as Dreamweaver negotiates the connection to your Web site.

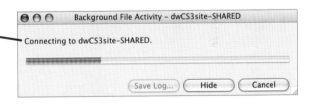

5 Once the connection is made, the remote site's files appear in the left side of the Files panel.

6 You're ready to upload your files.

upload multiple files

If this is the first upload to your Web site, you'll be publishing multiple files, including all the necessary images for your pages. (See extra bits on page 129.)

1 In the Local Files pane, click to select the top-level folder that contains all the files you want to upload (dwCS3_example_site in our example).

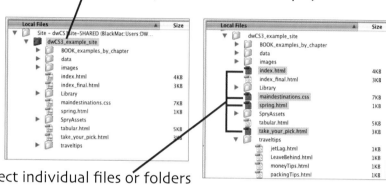

You also can select individual files or folders by Ctrl-clicking (Windows) or ⌘-clicking (Mac) them in the Local Files pane.

2 Drag the selected local files to the folder in the Remote Site pane or click the Put button to upload them.

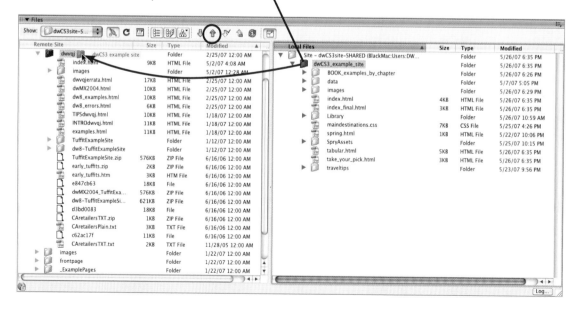

publish site

3 A series of progress dialog boxes flash by as Dreamweaver uploads the home page and all its dependent files. This may take several minutes to complete, depending on how many files you're uploading and the speed of your Internet connection.

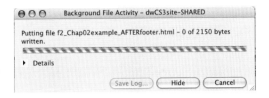

4 When the progress dialog boxes stop appearing, press the Refresh button…

5 …and then compare names of the Remote Site files to the names of your Local Files.

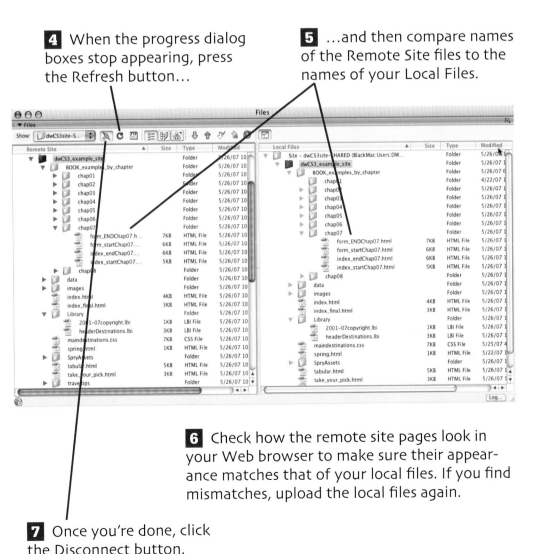

6 Check how the remote site pages look in your Web browser to make sure their appearance matches that of your local files. If you find mismatches, upload the local files again.

7 Once you're done, click the Disconnect button.

upload a single page

Sometimes you'll need to upload only a single page—for example, when you need to update information or fix a mistake.

1 Once you're connected, click the page file in the Local Files pane and drag it to the folder where the older version appears in the Remote Site pane.

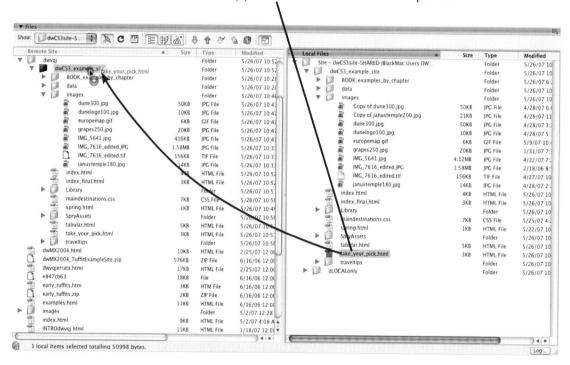

2 A single progress dialog box appears as Dreamweaver uploads the selected page. Use your Web browser to check the page on the remote Web site, and when you're done, click the Disconnect button.

extra bits

add search terms p. 118

- When picking keywords and a description, especially for an uncommon product or service, think of similar products or services and use words people would most likely type in to find them.

explore the files panel p. 121

- If you are working solo, the check-in/check-out system is cumbersome since it forces you to alert yourself that you're using a file. If, however, you're working solo and using multiple computers, say a desktop and a laptop, the checkout system helps keep all the files in synch.

- Sometimes it's tough to make room on the screen for a good view of your Web pages and the full Files panel, even on a large monitor. The easiest workaround is to arrange both just as you want them and press F8 to toggle the Files panel on or off.

set up remote site p. 123

- Check ahead with your Web site host to get the information needed for the Remote Info category. The great majority of sites use FTP to access sites, but asking ahead never hurts.

- Web-hosting firms usually email you a login name and password for posting your files. Keep the original email where you won't delete it and can find it later. If you ever buy a new computer, you'll need that password because Dreamweaver never reveals the password, just those black dots.

- If the test connection fails, double-check your entries in the Site Definition dialog box. Note that entries are case sensitive. Almost inevitably, you'll find a mistyped entry.

upload multiple files p. 126

- In step 2 of our example, the dwCS3_example_site folder is dragged and dropped into my site's existing dwvqj folder. The other files visible in the dwvqj folder were created for this book's previous edition covering Dreamweaver 8.

publish site

index

index

index

index

images (continued)
 optimizing, 26
 resampling, 26, 38, 44
 sharpening, 38
 storing, 44
 tools for working with, 26
 viewing information
  about, 26
Import Tabluar Data button, 57
Import Tabluar Data dialog
 box, 53
index.html file, 14, 24
Input Tag Accessibility
 Attributes dialog box,
 103, 104
Insert button, Assets tab, 115
Insert Column buttons, 49
Insert Flash Video dialog
 box, 30
Insert Jump Menu dialog box,
 99–100
Insert Row buttons, 47, 48, 51
Insert toolbar
 Common tab. See Common
  tab
 Common vs. Text setting, 24
 Data tab, 52
 expanding/collapsing, 3
 Forms tab, 99, 102
 Named Anchor button, 64
 and special characters, 24
interactivity, 93–108
 benefits of, 93
 with forms, 102–107, 108
 with jump menus,
  99–101, 108
 with navigation menus, ix,
  94–98, 108
internal links, viii, 59, 60–61, 75
Internet connections, 125, 127

J

JavaScript, 4, 94
Jump Menu button, 99
Jump Menu command, 108
jump menus, ix, 99–101, 108

K

keywords, 118, 129
Keywords dialog box, 118

L

labels
 field, 104, 107
 menu, 94, 96
layer-based layouts, 24
Layout CSS menu, 12
Layout tab, 4, 47, 49, 51
layouts
 frames-based, 24
 liquid, 12, 84
 pre-designed, 24
 style-sheet based, 24
 using tables to create, 45
.lbi files, 116
Library category button, Assets
 tab, 112
library items, 112–116
 and Assets tab, 109
 creating, 112–113
 editing, 114
 file suffix for, 116
 inserting, 115
 naming, 113
 previewing changes to, 114
 purpose of, ix, 112
 styling, 113, 116
 updating, 113
Link Checker tab, 120
link-related buttons, 59
link states, 70, 74
Link window, Property
 Inspector, 26, 62, 65,
 66, 120
links, 59–75
 anchor, 64–65, 75
 email, 63
 external, 59, 62, 75
 fixing broken, 120
 image, 66
 internal, 59, 60–61, 75

to items on other Web sites,
 59, 62
between pages on Web site,
 59, 60–61
purpose of, 59
setting colors/styles for,
 70–74, 75
testing, 61, 62, 63, 69
underlining, 71–72
visited vs. unvisited, 70
within Web pages, 64–65
liquid layouts, 12, 84
list styles, 82
list tags, 82
lists, ix, 21–22
local files, 121, 122
Local Files pane, 126, 128
local root folder, 7–8, 9
local site
 naming, 7, 9
 setting up, 7–8, 9
login name, 129
logos, 17
luggage-tag button, 118

M

Macintosh, text size and, 24
Map window, Property
 Inspector, 26, 67
menu bars, 94–98, 108
menu labels, 94, 96
menus
 drop-down, 4
 fly-out, 94
 horizontal vs. vertical, 108
 jump, ix, 99–101, 108
 navigation, ix, 94–98, 108
Merge Cells command, 50
meta data, 119
mouse-triggered items, 4
multiple-choice questions, 105

N

Named Anchor button/dialog
 box, 64, 65

index

W

WayWest.net, xii. *See also* companion Web site
Web browsers
  checking remote site pages in, 127, 128
  previewing forms in, 107
  previewing menus in, 96
  previewing video in, 30
  testing links in, 61, 62, 63, 69
  for visually impaired visitors, 44
Web-crawler programs, 63
Web-hosting firms, 129
Web pages. *See also* Web sites
  adding footers to, 23
  adding images to, 27–28. *See also* images
  adding interactivity to, 93–108. *See also* interactivity
  adding search terms to, 118–119
  adding tables to, 46–47, 57. *See also* tables
  adding text to, 15–16
  adding video to, 29–32
  advantages over printed pages, 93
  attaching style sheets to, 81
  choosing layout for, 12
  creating, 12–14
  creating headings for, 19–20
  creating lists in, 21–22
  detaching style sheets from, 80
  fixing mistakes in, 128
  importing tabular data into, 52–54
  inserting image placeholders in, 17–18
  linking, 60–61. *See also* links
  naming, 24
  natural flow for, 81
  preparing images for, 26
  publishing, 117, 126–128
  replacing image placeholders in, 40–41
  reusing items in, 109–116
  updating, 128
Web search engines, 118
Web servers, 117, 123
Web sites. *See also* Web pages
  adding navigation menu to, 94–98
  checking/fixing links in, 120
  creating home page for, 11–14, 24
  describing purpose of, 118
  linking pages in, 59, 60–61
  linking to items on other, 59, 62
  publishing, 117. *See also* publishing
  saving style sheet for, 13
  setting up local version of, 7–8, 9
  steps for creating, 12
  storing files for, 7
  this book's companion, vii, xii
  uploading files to, 126–128
widgets, 4, 94
Windows systems, text size on, 24
wrapping text, 42–43

GET UP AND RUNNING QUICKLY!

For more than 15 years, the practical approach to the best-selling *Visual QuickStart Guide* series from Peachpit Press has helped millions of readers—from developers to designers to systems administrators and more—get up to speed on all sorts of computer programs. Now with select titles in full color, *Visual QuickStart Guide* books provide an even easier and more enjoyable way for readers to learn about new technology through task-based instruction, friendly prose, and visual explanations.

Task-Based
Information is broken down into concise, one- and two-page tasks to help you get right to work.

Visual
Hundreds of screen shots illustrate the steps and show you the best way to do them.

Step by Step
Numbered, easy-to-follow instructions guide you through each task.

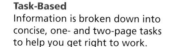

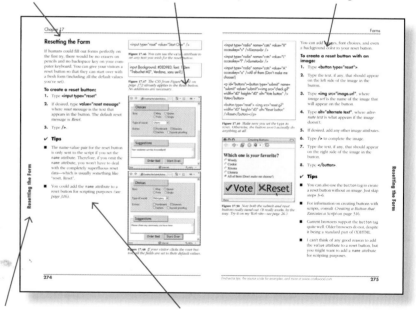

Quick Reference
Tabs on each page identify the task, making it easy to find what you're looking for.

Tips
Lots of helpful tips are featured throughout the book.